ECHOES OF A CENTURY
1864–1964

1864–1964

Echoes of a Century

The Centenary History of Southern Newspapers Limited

Compiled from the Company's records by
GORDON SEWELL

SOUTHAMPTON
1964

Made and printed in Great Britain by
The Camelot Press Ltd., London and Southampton

Contents

List of Illustrations

Foreword

BY SIR ROBERT PERKINS
Chairman, Southern Newspapers Limited

AS ONE WHOSE family has been closely associated with Southern Newspapers Limited during the whole of its 100 years' existence, it gives me particular pleasure to introduce this history which has been written to mark the firm's centenary.

From small beginnings we have grown into a great provincial newspaper enterprise, second to none in the South of England. This, I believe, has been achieved as a result of a sense of identity and purpose which has been shared over the years by directors, management and staff. Looking back across the past century, there can be few undertakings in our industry which have enjoyed such happy relations between employers and employed. Long may this tradition be maintained!

We began in the Victorian Age – indeed, through the old *Hampshire Advertiser* our roots go back to Georgian times – but it is this century which has witnessed the most exciting developments in the growth of our Company. There were, however, moments in the last war when it seemed doubtful whether we would even survive! Yet here we are, stronger than ever, with fine new headquarters in Southampton, our parent city, and new, rebuilt or expanded offices throughout our ever-growing territory.

When the Company was formed in 1864, nearly all newspapers in this country were party political organs, and the *Hampshire Advertiser* and the *Southern Echo*, in their early days, were no exception, as the reader of this history will discover for himself. But for many years our publications have pursued an independent policy, free of all party affiliations, and this they will continue to do. For us – as for C. P. Scott, perhaps the greatest provincial editor-proprietor of our time – "comment is free, but facts are sacred".

In compiling this history from the Company's records – such of them as survived the destruction of our head office in the war – and from the files of its various newspapers, Mr. Gordon Sewell, our chief leader-writer, has interwoven the story of Southern Newspapers Limited with that of outstanding events in Southampton and the neighbouring region. The result is a book which not only serves as the domestic chronicle of a provincial newspaper company, but also, I hope, makes a useful contribution to Press and regional history.

Robert Perkins

Acknowledgments

THANKS ARE DUE in the first place to Mr. R. R. Gleave, O.B.E., J.P., Director, General Manager and Editor-in-chief, who spent many hours going through the Company's records of the past quarter of a century in order to gather up material for the last four chapters of this book. Mr. Gleave's own memories of over forty years' association with the firm have helped to settle many a doubtful point and have enriched the narrative in several places.

The author has also drawn on the personal recollections of Mrs. E. Perkins, of Boldre Bridge House; and of Mr. R. I. Palmer, Director and Secretary, whose specialised knowledge of the records of Southern Newspapers Limited, and of the financial and legal aspects of the firm's history, have proved invaluable.

Among others to whom thanks are due special mention should be made of the following:

The editors of the Company's three evening newspapers – Mr. Rodney Andrew, J.P. (*Southern Evening Echo*), Mr. Douglas Sims (*Evening Echo, Bournemouth*) and Mr. A. R. Adlam, J.P. (*Dorset Evening Echo*); Mr. Douglas Gleave, Manager, *Evening Echo, Bournemouth*; Mr. Geoffrey O'Connor, Assistant Manager and Assistant Editor, *Southern Evening Echo*; Mr. H. F. S. Kimber, Advertisement Manager-in-chief, Southern Newspapers Limited; Mr. Denys Treseder, executive assistant, *Southern Evening Echo*; Mr. A. E. Rawlings, Sports Editor, *Southern Evening Echo*, and the late Mr. G. F. White, former Sports Editor; Mr. G. S. Raynes, chief librarian, *Southern Evening Echo*; Mr. James Adams, chief photographer, and Mr.

S. Weyman, chief process engraver, *Southern Evening Echo*, who assisted Mr. Gleave in preparing the illustrations for this book; the Borough Librarian of Falmouth for permission to reproduce the photograph of Passmore Edwards; Southampton Chamber of Commerce for permission to reproduce the photograph of Joseph R. Stebbing; the City Librarian of Southampton and the Librarian of the University of Southampton; Mr. S. Heather, who contributed impressions of the *Southern Echo* during World War I.

Much use has been made of the files of the Company's newspapers. Other publications and books which have provided facts or quotations include the Company's house journals, *Echograms* (Editor, C. F. Carr) and *Echoing Times* (Editor, G. W. O'Connor); *Southampton, the English Gateway*, by Bernard Knowles (Hutchinson); *Thirty-eight Years of Public Life in Southampton, 1910-1948*, by Sir Sidney Kimber; *History of Southampton University*, by A. Temple Patterson; "Walter Frank Perkins: a Memoir" by Mary Hopkirk (*Catalogue of the Walter Frank Perkins Agricultural Library*); *They Never Failed* (Newspaper Society); *Southampton Chamber of Commerce – A Brief History*, by Gordon Sewell; and *Collected Essays on Southampton* (Southampton Corporation).

G. S.

CHAPTER I

Beginnings

THE HAMPSHIRE ADVERTISER County Newspaper and
Printing and Publishing Company Limited – now Southern
Newspapers Limited – was incorporated on June 14, 1864, but
the story of this great provincial newspaper enterprise started
over forty years earlier, in 1823. On Monday, July 28 of that
year, the first copies of the *Southampton Herald and Isle of Wight
Gazette* came off the press – a large four-page sheet, closely
printed, carrying "foreign intelligence" and national news as
well as local reports, and containing a pompous leading article
in the tradition which Charles Dickens satirised when he
described the *Eatanswill Gazette* in *Pickwick Papers*. ("We are
devotedly attached to the Constitution, in Church and State.
Pro Rege, Grege, Lege is our motto. The Altar and the Throne
will be our landmark. To stem the torrent of sedition and
blasphemy, to diffuse the sentiments of loyalty, and to advocate
the cause of religion – the only true basis on which both public
peace and private happiness can rest – shall be the object
nearest to our heart.") The *Herald*'s publishers were Messrs.
E. Skelton & Son, booksellers and commercial printers, with
premises in Southampton's historic and elegant High Street –
No. 22, known as the Circulating Library. The first copies of
this new Tory county weekly were printed on a hand-press,
the ink for which was supplied by human "dabbers".

Three years later the Skeltons sold out to John Coupland, a
great name in the history of South of England journalism.
Under his vigorous direction, a new office was built, up-to-date

machinery installed, and the circulation of the paper became the largest in Hampshire. In 1827, ten years before Queen Victoria came to the throne, Coupland changed the title to that of the *Hampshire Advertiser*, under which name it continued to play its part in the life of the region until 1940, when its printing plant was destroyed by enemy action.

Coupland's successor was Robert Balfour King, whose name appears as the paper's publisher. It is not clear whether he was one of the proprietors, but he was certainly the business brains of the paper, and when it was taken over by the Hampshire Advertiser Company in 1864 the directors retained his services as Manager, a position he held until shortly before his death in 1877.

No more appropriate time could have been chosen for the formation of the new company, for in the middle of the nineteenth century the town was undergoing the latest of its several metamorphoses. The trade of the port had been of small consequence since Tudor times. Southampton enjoyed perhaps half a century of fame and prosperity as a spa during the Georgian Age, and the 1800's found it still notable as a watering-place. But its fortunes in this respect were declining when, in the decade which began in 1830, the town's economic situation was dramatically transformed by the coming of the railway and the building of the docks. Thanks to the power of steam, it was well on the way to becoming a great port again.

These changes were commented on in the Preface to the first official *Post Office Directory* to the town, published in 1843:

"Southampton has ceased to be a mere fashionable town, and is now filled with a permanently resident population principally engaged in commercial pursuits. The rise of Southampton into magnitude as a commercial town has been singularly rapid. It is now an undoubted fact that from the proximity of Southampton to London, and its railway communication with the Metropolis, it must always remain unrivalled as a provincial port for steamers conveying passengers to and from the

J. Passmore Edwards, founder of the *Southern Echo*.

Front page of the first issue of the *Hampshire Advertiser* to be published under the imprint of the Hampshire Advertiser Company Limited in 1864. It bears the date June 18 – four days after the Company was incorporated.

Clippings from the first edition of the *Southern Echo* (August 20, 1888)

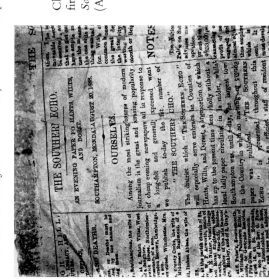

Channel Islands, the West Indies, the Continent (more especially in a few months hence, when the railway is completed between Rouen and Paris), the Peninsula, Mediterranean, East Indies and China.

"The realisation of this good fortune has caused, and must cause, the number of inhabitants in Southampton to increase to a remarkable extent. Houses, and even streets, rise up as if by magic in this prosperous and highly-favoured town, thereby rendering any enumeration of its inhabitants continually impossible. It is confidently believed, however, that this *Post Office Directory* will prove a most convenient and valuable work of reference for a very long period."

The foundations of the port's modern prosperity were laid during these fertile years. From the beginning the Dock Company had specialised in providing for the needs of the largest steamers, and by the 1860s the port was being used by some of the principal shipping lines of the day, British and foreign: the P. & O. and Royal Mail companies, the Union Line, the Hamburg-America and North German Lloyd, and the Vanderbilt Line. After the outbreak of the American Civil War, transatlantic mails began to pass through the port.

The businessman who, more than any other, realised the commercial potentialities of Southampton was Joseph R. Stebbing, first Chairman of the Hampshire Advertiser Company. He was a native of Portsmouth who had come to Southampton in the 1830s and set up in business as an optician and nautical instrument-maker. Later, Mr. A. Temple Patterson tells us, in his *History of Southampton University*, Stebbing became a ship's chandler, banker and director of various companies, playing a pioneering part in almost all aspects of the town's commercial and civic progress, and showing himself particularly alive to the importance of railway and dock development. Mr. Patterson continues:

"Supporting with equal energy everything which promoted the social welfare of the people, he took a keen interest in the Polytechnic Institution, of which he had now for many years

B

been the President. Genial, generous, and possessed of considerable powers of rough persuasive eloquence, he became successively a Town Councillor, Alderman and later Mayor; but it was probably as President of the Chamber of Commerce, in whose formation in 1851 he took a leading part and over which he presided almost continuously until 1867, that he exercised his greatest influence." (His grave is still regularly tended by the Chamber of Commerce of the present day.)

This, then, was the dynamic personality who played a leading part in the floating of the Advertiser Company, of which he remained Chairman until his death in 1874. His fellow directors were Walter Perkins, brother of Sir Frederick Perkins, a famous Mayor of this period, William Campbell, R. W. Simonds, and William Cooper. A small number of shareholders, nearly all local people, had invested £12,000 in £10 shares in the concern.

Almost immediately a committee of management was formed, consisting of all the directors except Mr. Cooper, the board explaining to the shareholders at the first annual meeting (September 14, 1865) that this had been done "to ensure the requisite attention to the important interests confided to their care . . .".

The enthusiasm with which the directors – all busy men – attended the *Advertiser* office must have astonished (and perhaps dismayed) Robert Balfour King. At a meeting of the board held on January 2, 1865, the Chairman reported that the sub-committee (as the committee of management was now known) had "held stated weekly meetings for the transaction of the business of the Company and occasionally other meetings in the week for special matters".

The first matter to occupy the attention of the committee of management, it seems, was the cost of the leading articles. These were not written by the Editor, J. D. Hubbarde, but by a specialist in political affairs. Whether he was a salaried member of the staff or an outside contributor is not clear, but whichever he was, in the opinion of the committee he was being overpaid for his work! The new directors showed their business acumen by making "a satisfactory arrangement with the gentleman engaged in that department for a payment of £100 per annum, thus effecting a saving of £50 per annum".

The Eatanswill pomposity of those first leaders in the *Southampton Herald* could no longer be detected in the editorial columns of the 1864 *Hampshire Advertiser*. Instead, we find well-informed comment pungently expressed. There is indeed a Churchillian note about what the paper had to say concerning the dispute over Schleswig-Holstein which led to the Prussian-Danish War: "So long as certain European Powers were under the impression that France and England would unite to prevent or punish acts of spoliation, so long were those Powers restrained within the limits of decency. But no sooner had Earl Russell made his now too notorious declaration, that under no circumstances would England go to war for Poland or, indeed, in defence of any aggrieved State or people, than those Powers threw off the very flimsy restraint they had already respected, and proceeded to their work of conquest in the real old style of Frederick 'the Great' or of Catherine. . . ."

The Conservatives, in opposition since 1859, were at this time planning afresh the political strategy which would bring them electoral victory two years hence, in 1866. "What the Conservative chiefs desire", explained the *Hampshire Advertiser* leader-writer, "is to complete the reconstruction of their party upon a broad national basis. The people of England have had enough of Whigs and Whiggery. The Conservative chiefs desire to recruit their strength from the ranks of those moderate men of all classes who act as ballast of the vessel of State."

These excerpts have been quoted to give the reader some idea of the political flavour of the *Advertiser* in those days. But all the evidence indicates that the directors of the new company, though staunch supporters of the Tory cause, were at this time more interested in the business than in the political aspects of their newspaper undertaking. In the first Annual Report we read that the attention of Messrs. Stebbing, Perkins, Campbell, Simonds and Cooper was "occupied at an early date with the consideration of the great loss and inconvenience arising from a separation of the Job Printing from the Newspaper Printing – one being carried on in York Buildings and the other in the premises in High Street – and an opportunity offering of taking suitable adjoining premises – part of Mr. Cooksey's stores – your Directors have made a very valuable addition to the High Street Printing Office, now forming one of the most complete Printing Offices in Hampshire."

During this first year in the Company's history £150 was spent on improving and increasing the stock of type, and £147 (obtained from the late proprietors, after considerable negotiation) on putting the main premises into "proper and tenantable repair". At the same time, salaries were increased: that of R. B. King (described in the Board minutes as "Secretary, Manager and Publisher") from £3 per week to £200 a year; that of J. D. Hubbarde, the Editor, from £3 to £3 10s. a week. The salary of Mr. J. D. Collett, sub-editor and reporter, was raised from £2 2s. to £2 10s. a week, and that of Mr. Moore, the head of the Job Printing Office, from 25s. to 30s. a week. (The value of money, it must be remembered, was then many times what it is today.)

Expenses, it was clear, were going to increase, and the profits from the *Hampshire Advertiser* were modest. The directors placed their hopes in commercial printing, and sought increased business from those most likely to be interested – the shareholders of the Company! "Your Directors are most anxious to impress the important subject of job printing on your attention and – having now such complete and convenient Printing Offices, and type of the newest and most suitable description – urge upon you to use your influence in sending printing to the Company's Offices, where it can be done as well, as cheaply, and as expeditiously as at any office in the County. Attention, on the part of the proprietors, to this branch, would give a large additional dividend. At present you have not anything like the amount of printing which your exertions may command, and the influence of the Newspaper ought to ensure...."

No criticism of staff or management was implied, however. The directors expressed "satisfaction with the services of Mr. King and Mr. Hubbarde, in the management of the Paper, and generally with the good conduct of the staff engaged thereon". They had made "as few changes as possible in the general management of the business purchased by you, as they thought it prudent not to make much change in the conduct of a Paper which had gained so influential a position. They trust, however, that the amount of careful supervision they have been enabled to bestow upon it, has been calculated to improve that position and the future prospects of the Paper."

The financial situation of the new company was, to say the least, satisfactory. After the first year's trading a dividend of 10 per cent. clear of income tax was recommended on the capital paid up. This absorbed £778 17s. 4d., leaving a sum of £150 to be set aside for depreciation "and for the payment of such an allowance to the Directors as you consider their exertions fairly entitle them to". (A year or two later, directors' fees amounted to £200 per annum.)

Further light on the financial arrangements of the Company in those early days is shed by the board's appeal to "those shareholders who have not yet paid the four-fifths, agreed upon at the preliminary general meetings, to do so as soon as possible". It was explained that the purchase of the business had been a cash transaction, and that the withholding of payment of calls had been a source of considerable inconvenience to the directors, "especially as they felt reluctant to put into force the powers of forfeiture of shares, for non-payment of calls, which the Articles of Association confer upon them".

However, we find no further talk of reluctance to pay up, for it soon became obvious that the shareholders had invested their money in a good thing. At the second annual meeting (September 17, 1866) they learnt that "the operations of the company are increasingly remunerative, showing additional profit on the one hand and a reduction of debts due by the company on the other". In fact, the entire indebtedness of the firm at this time was less than £100. The capital account was "practically closed" with a balance of £1,105 11s. 9d. "not at present required to be called up"; and the Company's premises in York Buildings had been let on lease at the "satisfactory rental" of £40 a year.

The Statement of Accounts for the year ending June 30, 1866, tells us so much about the early history of the company that it must be given in some detail:

Capital A/C

Receipts	£	s.	d.
Total amount of capital in £10 shares . .	12,000	–	–
140 paid-up Shares to Vendors as part payment	1,400	–	–
Calls and instalments received on 1,060 £10 shares	8,326	13	4
Amount paid in excess of calls made . .	240	–	–
Amount not yet paid on calls made . .	153	6	8
Balance of capital not yet called up . .	1,880	–	–

Disbursements			
Amount paid to vendors as per agreement .	10,000	–	–
Legal and other preliminary expenses in forming the Company	299	16	–
New type and printing press for jobbing office	156	14	10
Alterations, repairs, rearrangement of buildings and furniture	437	17	5

Trading A/C

Receipts   £   s.   d.

Amount received for advertisements, printing
and papers 5,608 15 11

Disbursements

	£	s.	d.
Rent and taxes	218	11	2
Wages and salaries	1,810	4	2
London papers	26	13	5
Postage	35	9	10
Reporters' expenses	17	11	5
Railway parcels	41	19	7
Printing materials, coal, etc., printing offices.	169	15	6
Correspondence	247	19	—
Stationery, printing paper, etc. . . .	52	12	—
Stamps and blanks for newspaper . .	1,740	16	7
Gas	37	8	1
Income and assessed taxes	28	10	6
Insurance	28	8	6
Dividends	778	17	4
Directors' fees	200	—	—
Secretary's salary, auditors' fees and gratuities	89	2	—

During the remainder of the 60s the Company continued to prosper. But, in the opinion of the board, the shareholders were still not backing up the commercial printing department as they should. In the annual report for 1867 we read: "Your Directors again call your attention to the importance of aiding them in their efforts to increase the business of Job Printing and Stationery; with such a Proprietary, and the influence of the Paper, an additional 5 per cent. ought to be earned from this source alone, but your Directors feel that the Shareholders are not yet doing their utmost in influencing parties to employ the Company for this purpose. Your Directors also ask their Proprietors to aid them in obtaining advertisements for the London Papers, a business they have pressed into an increasing profit, and which the Shareholders could considerably influence."

This rebuke – for that is what it amounted to – did not have the desired effect, for in the next year we find the directors expressing their regret that "the Shareholders generally do not exert themselves in obtaining Job Printing for this Company; by attention to this they might ensure a much larger dividend".

The biggest change which occurred during the latter years of this decade was the publication of a mid-week edition of the *Advertiser* at 1d. The paper, like its Whig rival, the *Hampshire Independent*, had for many years been published on Saturdays, price 2d. The decision to issue a mid-week edition at half that price seems to have been taken in response to the competition of the recently established Radical weekly, the *Southampton Times*. At first a take-over bid was contemplated. But after Mr. King and Mr. Hubbarde had been consulted at a meeting of the management committee (January 15, 1869), the directors decided "not to treat for the purchase of the *Southampton Times*". (The copyright of that paper was bought by the Company in 1925.)

Readers of the *Advertiser* sensed that important changes were in the wind when they read the following announcement: "Arrangements are now being entered into for making a very material alteration of the *Hampshire Advertiser* County Newspaper and due notice will be given as soon as they are perfected. We anticipate that the new arrangement will meet with the concurrence and entire approbation of the great Conservative Party throughout the country."

Later that month, a general meeting of the shareholders approved the new policy. In future the Company was to publish "the present supplement to the *Hampshire Advertiser* on Wednesday in each week as a mid-weekly paper at 1d., and the Paper-in-chief on Saturday at 2d., both papers to be improved as far as possible – the type smaller in some respects, local reports lessened so far as it could be suitably done, advertisements put in small type, and privileges given to large and stated terms advertisers, with reduction on those in the mid-weekly paper. The advisability of having a general and local leader in the last-named paper was considered. . . ."

It was a daring experiment which paid off. At the fifth annual meeting, held that year (September 6, 1869), the directors reported that "notwithstanding that . . . the Paper has been reduced in price, and the Supplement published as a Mid-Weekly Paper . . . the Ordinary Dividend of 10 per cent. can be paid". Cautiously, they added the rider that it was "not yet clear that the reduction in price and continuance of a Mid-Weekly Paper will enable the payment of so large a Dividend on future occasions; your Directors will, however, use every exertion and practice every economy to ensure as large a Dividend as possible." They were as good as their word!

CHAPTER 2

Mid-Victorian Southampton

HERE LET US pause a moment to take a closer look at South-ampton in the mid-Victorian era which saw the birth of the Hampshire Advertiser Company.

New suburbs were springing up on all sides, as the big estates on the town's outskirts – Banister's, Bevois Mount and Bellevue – were broken up and developed. To quote from an advertisement for one of the development companies, "South-ampton has wonderfully increased in size and importance with-in the last ten years. The want of new houses is much felt." (Plots on the Avenue Estate ranged in price from £44 to £400.)

Millbrook parish, which included the rapidly growing district of Shirley, had quadrupled its population in less than thirty years, and the Shirley Conveyance Company (remote ancestor of the Corporation transport system) ran about forty horse omnibuses a day to and from the town. New streets were going up at Portswood and on the eastern bank of the Itchen. Most of these were middle-class developments, and included many substantial homes for the families of those professional men, merchants, sea captains and managers whose numbers and influence were transforming the character of a once aristocratic resort.

There was, unfortunately, another and less pleasing side to Southampton's growth and commercial progress in the 60s. As the working-class population expanded, it was housed in rapidly erected terraces in St. Mary's parish and in Northam, and these were built with little regard for the health of their inhabitants. Many of the sites chosen were swampy, and when the cholera epidemic attacked Southampton in the summer of 1866 the cases were chiefly in these "ill-ventilated, low, dirty localities". The worst slums were to be found in an area consisting of about half a square mile, which included the courts and alleys at the back of the High Street and in Kingsland.

But it must not be supposed that all the men of influence and authority in Southampton at that time were indifferent to social needs. The Local Board of Health, taking over from the insolvent Improvement Commissioners, repaired the roads, modernised the sewerage system and improved the town's water supply.

Judged by modern standards, these achievements may sound sufficiently modest. In the context of the age, they were almost revolutionary. And since it was a Tory "revolution", we may be sure that the *Hampshire Advertiser* played an important part in it. What happened is related by Miss Patricia Morris in the chapter on the mid-nineteenth century which she contributed to *Collected Essays on Southampton*:

"Bred in the tradition of a sturdy individualism, associated with the doctrine that public bodies seldom spend their money as wisely as private individuals, the Liberal Councillors of Southampton were slow to read the signs of the time. While they were considering the problem, the Tories took action. They distrusted the Radicals' ability to govern the town and believed that it would be advantageous to bring Southampton under the Public Health Act, by which they hoped that local administration would be organised and controlled by the central Board of Health. A group of them, headed by Captain Engledue, the Superintendent of the Peninsular and Oriental Company, who was horrified by the insanitary conditions under which some of his company's employees were living, petitioned the General Board of Health for an inquiry. The result was the adoption of the Public Health Act in Southampton."

As the dominant party on the Council, the Radicals were obliged to administer the new Act, which they had strongly opposed. The new measures proved expensive and, as rates increased, cost the Radicals some of their popularity. But this was only a temporary reverse. In the 50s the Liberals were at the height of their power in Southampton, and the Tories – apart from the *Advertiser*'s first Chairman, Joseph Stebbing ("who was everyone's adviser on commercial questions", says Miss Morris), were mainly new and untried men.

The end of the decade saw the beginning of the Liberal decline. The party, locally, had become too closely identified with unpopular railway interests, and by the time our story opens Southampton was under Tory rule. Probably the formation of a newspaper company to promote an established organ of Conservative opinion could only have taken place in a period of Tory ascendancy and commercial success. (If a similar company had been formed in the 50s, it might have purchased the Liberal *Independent*. By an odd quirk of Fate that paper too was to be taken over by the Hampshire Advertiser Company before the century was out.)

The 70s brought with them a new anxiety for the directors of the company. As they informed the shareholders at the annual meeting in September, 1870, by means of stringent economy they had been able to establish a 1*d*. mid-week edition without "any serious diminution of profit". But now the local contemporary, whose competitive methods had forced the Advertiser Company to take this drastic step, was bringing out a *daily* newspaper[1] – the first to be published in Southampton. Should the Company take up this further challenge and establish a rival daily of its own?

The idea was considered, only to be rejected decisively. The directors confidently prophesied that the new paper would involve its proprietors in heavy losses and would have a short life. They were right. The time was not yet ripe for a successful

[1] Presumably the *Evening Star*, whose plant Passmore Edwards was to acquire when he started the *Southern Echo* in 1888.

daily in Southampton; in fact, nearly twenty years were to elapse before this became economically possible. It was in 1888 that the *Southern Echo* was established.

In any case, the Company could not consider a new venture at a time when it had just lost its most experienced editorial executive. After a long period of ill-health, Hubbarde had died leaving the *Advertiser* without an editor. The board expressed its gratitude to one "who had been so long a faithful and talented servant of the Paper". It is not clear from the records who succeeded him, but it appears that for a time, at any rate, Robert Balfour King combined editorial and managerial responsibilities. Certainly King stepped into the breach during the Editor's illness. The annual report for 1869 mentions that the long illness of Mr. Hubbarde had thrown "some additional labour" on Mr. King and some others of the staff." Under these circumstances, it was "pleasing to record how valuable have been the services of Mr. King, and how cheerfully he and the employees generally have discharged very onerous duties".

The records tell us little concerning Editor Hubbarde, but such glimpses as we are afforded leave an impression of an able journalist – one who carried his paper through a difficult period of transition when new proprietors were in control and competition was increasing. Only on one occasion was he found wanting, and that was when he allowed a libel to slip into the paper. He would have been unique among editors if he had never failed in this respect, but that was evidently not realised by the directors, who were of the opinion that Hubbarde should have "struck out of the article those parts which were in all probability of a libellous nature".

Perhaps the Editor was not sufficiently aware of the extent of his powers in this respect. Or of the legal responsibility which undoubtedly devolved upon him. In order that there should be no such misunderstandings in future, the directors – at a board meeting on January 17, 1866 – "unanimously resolved that power be given to Mr. Hubbarde to reject, alter, vary or remove any and every article or communication sent to the paper, or handed to him from or by any party whatsoever, which he may consider of a libellous nature''.

The 70s were a time of increasing costs and rising wages, a fact mentioned in nearly every annual report of the Company published during this period. But the 10 per cent. dividend was maintained, and in 1874 the directors claimed that "notwithstanding the continued advance in the price of materials and the rise in wages, the accounts presented would have shown a larger balance available for dividend than on any previous occasion, had not upwards of £400 been expended on a new two-feeder Machine", thus providing "the alternative of a second Machine in the event of one breaking down at a critical moment".

The tenth anniversary of the Company, however, was marred by sad news. The annual report went on to refer with "extreme sorrow" to "the decease of the late Chairman of the Company, Mr. J. R. Stebbing, who has been removed from a life of active usefulness, not only to this Company, but to his fellow townsmen. Mr. Stebbing had acted as Chairman of the Company from its establishment, and had always been of eminent service to its interests, from the valuable advice he was able to afford."

His place was taken by Mr. George Dunlop, a wealthy man who had succeeded Stebbing as President of the local Chamber of Commerce. (When the Association of Chambers of Commerce held its Annual Conference at Southampton in 1872, the delegates were 'munificently entertained' by Dunlop, who seems to have been an important social figure as well as an influential businessman.) Dunlop took the place of R. W. Simonds on the board.

J. E. Le Feuvre had joined the board at about the same time as Dunlop, having been elected to fill the vacancy left by the resignation of William Campbell. This somewhat controversial figure was destined to be Mayor of the town and President of the Chamber. In 1866 the directors were singing his praises: "Mr. Le Feuvre's colleagues desire to state that after several months' experience of that gentleman's ability and assistance

they feel great satisfaction with the selection they have made."
And for the next nine years they saw no reason to change their
minds. In 1875, however, Le Feuvre and his fellow-directors
quarrelled, and Le Feuvre resigned from the board.

Politics – and perhaps an element of personal vanity – were at
the root of the trouble. Mr. Le Feuvre had written a letter to
the *Advertiser* which the Editor, acting on the Chairman's
instructions, refused to publish. Le Feuvre's version of the row
is given in the following letter of resignation which he wrote
to George Dunlop:

"November 4, 1875

"I am very strongly impressed with the injury inflicted on
the town by the exaggerated statements as to its rating being
made by public men and reported in the newspapers. On
Wednesday last the *Hampshire Advertiser* reported a speech
made by a candidate for the office of Town Councillor containing some most extravagant statements as regards its rating
at the present time. Having long taken an interest in the financial affairs of the town, occupying also the position of Deputy
Chairman of the Finance Committee, I thought it my duty to
forward a letter to the Editor of the *Hampshire Advertiser*,
pointing out the actual amount of our rating and showing that
it was considerably less than as stated in the speech referred to.

"You have informed me that as Chairman of the Board you
gave orders that this letter should not be inserted, on the
grounds that the statements made therein were likely to prove
damaging to the Party supported by the Paper contesting the
representation of the town in the Council. I have no desire now
to complain of your action personally in this matter, and
accept the treatment of my letter as an intimation that, however erroneous may be the statements made by a political
partisan, and however damaging these may be to the town
generally, the policy of the Paper is deliberately to suppress a
correct representation of the facts if there is reason to believe
that more votes may be secured by allowing the original
statement to remain uncontradicted.

"Such a policy I cannot regard otherwise than as unjust and ungenerous, and however triumphant for the moment must surely, as dishonest, prove ultimately unsuccessful. In any case, having regard to the duty to and respect for myself, I cannot by continuing a member of the board sanction it; and therefore beg to tender my resignation as director of the Company."

Unjust, ungenerous, dishonest . . . these were surprisingly harsh terms for a man to apply to a newspaper which he had helped to direct for nearly a decade. Unfortunately, Dunlop's side of the question was not recorded. But the fact that the board unanimously decided to accept Le Feuvre's resignation suggests that their confidence in their Chairman was unshaken.

The opportunity was taken to reward Robert Balfour King, now an old man, for long and loyal service. He was elected to fill the vacancy, thus becoming the firm's first Managing Director. Only a few months previously the board had resolved that "Mr. King, who had been in the establishment from boyhood to the present time, a period of 49 years", should retire on pension, and that "he should look for some practical and efficient person to bring in and instruct in the business of the office and succeed him as manager". The minutes record that Mr. King thanked the directors for their consideration and kindness, and promised to conform to their wishes, but respectfully declined becoming a pensioner on the establishment.

He did not live long to enjoy his new office, for at their monthly meeting on May 3, 1877, the directors "recorded deep regret at the death of Mr. Robert Balfour King and their sense of the valuable services which he for so many years had rendered to the Company."

His son, Henry King, who had been with the firm for nine years, succeeded him as manager at a salary of £150 a year, £50 a year less than R.B.K. had been paid in 1865. This modest sum suggests that, to begin with, the appointment was tentative and that young King was regarded as being on trial. He soon proved his worth, and when he in turn became

Joseph R. Stebbing
(1864-74)

*Walter Perkins
(1888-1901)

W. Frank Perkins
(1901-32)

Sir Russell Bencraft, J.P.
(1932-43)

W. A. Gleave, J.P.
(1943-5)

Sir Robert Perkins
(1945-   )

*George Dunlop was the second Chairman, 1874-88, but no portrait of him has survived.

1

2

3

THE PRESENT BOARD OF
DIRECTORS

1 Sir Robert Perkins (Chairman)

2 Colonel G. F. Perkins,
C.B.E., D.S.O. (Deputy
Chairman)

3 P. J. B. Perkins

4 R. R. Gleave, O.B.E., J.P.
(General Manager and Editor-
in-chief)

5 R. I. Palmer (Secretary)

4

5

Rodney Andrew, J.P.
(Deputy General
Manager and Editor,
Southern Evening Echo)

H. F. S. Kimber
(Advertisement
Manager-in-chief)

D. A. Gleave
(Manager, *Evening
Echo, Bournemouth*)

A. B. Burnett
(Manager, *Dorset
Evening Echo*)

L. Udall
(London Manager)

G. W. O'Connor
(Assistant Manager
and Assistant Editor,
Southern Evening Echo)

P. D. Treseder
(Executive Assistant,
Southern Evening Echo)

D. H. Sims
(Editor, *Evening
Echo, Bournemouth*)

A. R. Adlam, J.P.
(Editor, *Dorset
Evening Echo*)

Colonel Sir E. K. Perkins,
C.B.E., D.L., J.P.

J. C. Moberly

Harry Parsons, J.P.

Captain A. E. Jones, M.C.

Alderman R. C. Chambers,
J.P.

S. E. Whitehead, O.B.E.,
J.P.

Managing Director some thirty years later, his salary of £1,150 a year must have been one of the largest paid in provincial journalism at that time. His managership, as we shall see, covered some of the most important years of growth in the Company's first century.

Incidentally, when Henry King was appointed Manager the question of engaging a Secretary ("at a salary not exceeding £100 a year") was discussed. The directors were still looking for a suitable accountant to fill this office a year later. They were unsuccessful, and Henry King combined the secretarial duties with his own.

Robert Balfour King's death left a vacancy on the board, and this – ironically enough – was filled by none other than J. E. Le Feuvre. Evidently there had been a reconciliation!

As a party newspaper, published at a time when, in Gilbert's words, "every boy and every girl born into this world alive" was "either a little Liberal or else a little Conservative", the *Hampshire Advertiser*'s views were as important as its news. The man who for many years had been responsible for presenting them to the public was C. W. Francis, the leader-writer, whose death in 1879 left a gap on the paper which the directors had some difficulty in filling. At first they considered ordering leaders from the Central Press Agency in London, but wisely decided that the articles should be written in the office. This task was given to Mr. Collett, the Editor, whose salary was raised from £3 10s. to £4 a week in consequence.

As the decade drew to a close – in June, 1879, to be precise – the possibility of making a take-over bid for the *Southampton Observer* was discussed – and turned down. The financial position of the Company was stronger than ever. Property adjoining the High Street premises had been bought for £5,149 (raised by sale of stock and a loan from the bank) and, in addition to the usual 10 per cent. dividend, the board had sanctioned the issue of a 2½ per cent. bonus. This was only half the bonus paid in 1878, but the Company's assets had been strengthened.

c

CHAPTER 3

The Railway Age

A GLANCE AT the *Hampshire Advertiser* file for January, 1880, reminds us that these were anxious days for England. Memories of the Zulu War were fresh in men's minds (Southampton was the port of embarkation for South Africa) and the Afghan War was drawing to a close. "The year 1879", wrote a correspondent, "will long be remembered as the culmination of agricultural disaster unexampled during the present generation." The paper warned its readers that "Russia has again become the disturbing element" in international affairs, and complained that a group of Russian refugees, repudiated by the Tsar's Embassy in London, was being maintained in Southampton at the ratepayers' expense. From Ireland came news of sedition and distress among the peasantry.

Coming nearer home, the *Advertiser* managed to squeeze a little comfort from the *Annual Review of the Shipping Trade*, which reported, for the first time in four years, cheerfulness in shipping circles founded on a "steady, solid improvement in business generally, and what may be not unreasonably considered a positive termination of the settled gloom and stagnation in trade all round which, for a weary time, seemed to bar all hope of change for the better". But this optimism was not borne out by events. The early 80s witnessed idle shipyards and rising unemployment. Locally the depression was increased by the transfer of the P. & O. Line to London in 1881. This was a severe blow to Southampton's pride, for the P. & O. Company was the first important shipping line to use South-

ampton Docks when they were opened in the 40s. Nevertheless, schemes for new deep-water and graving docks went
ahead: the London and South Western Railway, which was to
give financial backing to the Dock Company, and eventually
take it over, had plenty of confidence in Southampton's
future.

Annual reports during the 80s contained frequent references
to the "depression in all branches of trade", yet the Company
continued to flourish. The dividend, it is true, went as low as
6 per cent., but the assets were growing and the *Advertiser*
seems to have had no difficulty in maintaining its position as the
most widely read county newspaper in Hampshire. Unfortunately, no record of the actual weekly circulation figure at this
time has survived. But a hint was given in the issue of January
3, 1880:

"Circulation of the Hampshire Advertiser"

"When the Newspaper Stamp was issued by the Government a return was published annually, showing the number of
stamps supplied to each newspaper, and we were in the habit
of publishing the figures referring to the local Newspapers in
this neighbourhood. The following was the number of penny
stamps issued to the undermentioned Papers for one year when
the Government return was made:

Hampshire Advertiser	67,000
Hampshire Telegraph	37,500
Hampshire Chronicle	30,750
Hampshire Independent . . .	25,494

"Since the abolition of the Newspaper Stamp, and the
introduction of the Halfpenny Wrapper, the circulation of the
Hampshire Advertiser has considerably increased and in order to
give our readers some idea of the present position, we have
gone through our books with the view to ascertaining the
number of Halfpenny Wrappers supplied to us during 12
months by the Post Office for the purpose of despatching our
Paper to subscribers in the County. The result shows that from

September 30, 1878 to September 30, 1879 the number was
84,120. Of course the quantity of Halfpenny wrappers used
gives no idea of the actual circulation, but it is generally acknowledged that the Paper which is in the habit of despatching
large numbers of copies through the Post has the largest
circulation among Families in the County and district in which
it is published.''

What follows is guesswork, but if we reckon the total
circulation as ten times the number sold to postal subscribers,
that gives us a weekly sale of approximately 16,000 copies – an
excellent figure for a provincial weekly in those days, and
rather more than double the 7,000 a week figure given in the
Post Office Guide for 1864. The limiting factor was still illiteracy;
the first fruits of the 1870 Education Act were to be harvested
by the $\frac{1}{2}d$. evening papers which began to appear at the end of
this decade – as we shall see.

So far as the Company and its weekly journal were concerned,
the big issue of this period was the controversy over the Didcot,
Newbury and Southampton Railway, a controversy which
brought about – for the second time – the resignation of Mr.
Le Feuvre from the *Hampshire Advertiser*'s board of directors.

The matter was raised at a meeting of the board held on
February 24, 1882, when Mr. Le Feuvre "brought forward
the subject of the New Railway Scheme and suggested the
Advertiser should continue to support the Didcot and Newbury
Railway and that an article should appear in the next edition of
the *Advertiser* advocating the same''.

The board hesitated about committing itself, though a little
later it was to come out strongly in favour of the Didcot
scheme. On this occasion Mr. J. D. Collett, the Editor, was
"instructed to write an article dealing with the discussion at the
Chamber of Commerce meeting and the two petitions that are
being signed in reference to the South Western Bill and the
Didcot and Newbury Bill, stating the two petitions are before
the ratepayers and they should decide for themselves which
would be most beneficial to the town''.

At the next board meeting, in March, the matter came up again, and the directors resolved to "adopt the policy of extending the railway facilities of the town and to assist by all means in their power the promotion of the Didcot, Newbury and Southampton Railway" by urging support of the scheme in the columns of the *Hampshire Advertiser*.

Mr. Le Feuvre, a shareholder of the Didcot Railway, must have been well satisfied, but developments were to take place which would cause him to break with the *Advertiser*. The Didcot faction wanted the Town Council to agree to £50,000 of ratepayers' money being invested in their scheme, and this was vigorously opposed by those who thought it an improper use of public funds. When it was suggested that a petition against this proposal had been signed almost entirely by persons in the employment of the "monopolistic" London and South-Western Railway, the superintendent of the Line at Southampton immediately sent a categorical denial to the *Advertiser*: "I beg to inform you that the statement is utterly untrue. On reference to the petition itself, it will be seen that it bears the signatures of a great number of principal merchants and others in the town, and I am in a position to prove that the whole of the signatures were obtained in a legitimate and proper manner."

Mr. Le Feuvre evidently felt that he had been placed in a false position, and so resigned his directorship of the *Hampshire Advertiser*. Two years later he was still fighting the battle of the Didcot Railway. At its half-yearly meeting, reported on March 19, 1884, he regretted that there were not sufficient funds in hand to enable the line to be completed, though he had no doubt that once it reached Southampton Docks it would prove highly profitable.[1]

This was the Age of Railway Mania in which fortunes were

[1] The Didcot and Newbury Railway was not the only local enterprise short of capital at this time. At the half-yearly meeting of the Southampton Dock Company in 1884 the Chairman, Mr. Steuart Macnaghten, said that if only the 70,000 inhabitants of Southampton would put up £7,000, the plans for a new deep-water dock could soon be carried into effect.

lost by crazy rivalries, and when the L. & S.W.R. and Great Western entered into an agreement to "avoid the foolish contests and absurd competition of the past", the *Advertiser* rejoiced. The arrangement, it said, would promote the public interest and convenience.

Returning to the Company's domestic affairs, we find convincing evidence of the growth of the firm. For twenty years it had operated from the original premises taken over in 1864, when the Hampshire Advertiser Company was formed, but now these were no longer adequate. So, at the board meeting held in February, 1884, the Manager "reminded the directors that the time was drawing in when the possession of the new premises would be required" – he was referring to No. 29 High Street, the next-door premises, purchased in 1879 – "and suggested that steps should be taken with regard to building a new Printing Office and laying out premises ready for occupation". These proposals had evidently been discussed more than once previously, for Henry King was immediately instructed to see Mr. Udall, the builder, and arrange for plans of a suitable building to be prepared for the board.

In the issue of April 2, 1884, readers were prepared for the coming changes by a bold announcement at the top of the leader column under the heading "Enlargement of the *Hampshire Advertiser*". The paper was shortly to be published in "an enlarged and improved form, so as more effectively to meet the increased requirements of the times". This had been rendered necessary by the ever-growing pressure on space from both news and advertisements. By the beginning of May the company would be able to offer the public a newspaper in size, type and general appearance second to none in the South of England. The Saturday edition was to be enlarged from forty-eight to fifty-six columns, and both the Saturday and Wednesday editions would be printed on larger sheets. The paper would be printed in an entirely new and improved type and nothing would be wanting to render it, in its enlarged form, "most acceptable to all classes of the community".

In order to carry out these plans new premises had been acquired adjoining the present offices, where a new and capacious printing office was in the course of erection. When completed these printing works would rank among the most commodious and up-to-date to be found outside London.

Henry King must be given much of the credit for this programme of renewal and expansion. It was he who urged the purchase of new type for the newspaper, "the present having been in use fifteen years and become much worn . . ." And it was he who recommended that the size of the *Advertiser* should be increased from six to seven columns a page. When Mr. Perkins suggested that the paper should be made up in "more but smaller pages, similar to the *Dorset County Chronicle*", it was King who fought, successfully, to retain "the old form in which the *Advertiser* had appeared for so many years".

One suspects that it was on his recommendation that the board purchased a new Otto Silent gas engine when the boiler of the old engine proved defective. Like a good Victorian, he believed in moving with the times; but so, for that matter, did the directors.

To quote the report for 1884, a considerable outlay was incurred in moving into and fitting up the new premises. But, added the directors when addressing the shareholders in the following year, "although the amount thus expended has been somewhat large, the Company now possesses a very valuable Property. A New Machine has been purchased of Messrs. Dawson and Sons, and is working in a very satisfactory manner, and your Directors have pleasure in stating that the whole Establishment has been removed, the Premises completed, and now form most extensive and convenient Printing and Publishing Offices, unsurpassed by any similar establishment in the South of England."

As the principal Tory paper in Hampshire, the *Advertiser*, with its middle-class readership, was preaching very largely to the converted, and in November, 1884, proposals were made by the County Conservative Association for reducing the price in order to attract more working-class readers. Delicate negotiations were entered into with the board by the Association's representative, Mr. W. H. Davis, who hinted that if the directors were prepared to reduce the price of the Saturday edition to 1*d*., the Association might guarantee an increase in circulation or reimburse the company for any losses that might be incurred, "the object being to render the paper more serviceable to the Party by circulating more extensively among the working-classes".

The board was naturally interested in the possibility of increasing the *Advertiser*'s circulation and influence, but was reluctant to take any step which might weaken its freedom of action. So it postponed making a decision, and appointed Messrs. Perkins and Cooper to meet Mr. Davis and talk the matter over. A month later the Manager reported that he had seen Mr. Davis, who was of the opinion that "the whole matter had better stand over for the present, as in consequence of the passing of the Redistribution of Seats Bill the circumstances would be altered and the Conservative committee would have to further consider the subject".

Though Mr. Davis now fades out of the picture, the Conservatives made a fresh approach in the following year through Lord Henry Scott, who wrote to the Company strongly urging it to reduce the price of the Saturday edition to 1*d*. The directors invited him to meet them for a full discussion, but there is no record of what the outcome was. The probability is that the matter was eventually dropped when it became apparent that, in order to meet growing competition, the company would have to enter the $\frac{1}{2}d$. evening newspaper business. But that is the subject of our next chapter.

As a paper pledged to defend constitutional principles, the *Advertiser* had been appealed to by the Conservatives. During the same period a local clergyman made these same principles the pretext for severely criticising the conduct of the publishers in a certain respect. He was the Rev. H. H. Pereira, Rector of St. Lawrence's Church, in whose parish the *Advertiser* office was situated. In May, 1884, he addressed the following letter to the board:

"I desire to draw your attention to two years Minister's dues which the Hants Advertiser Company are in arrears to me, up to September last. Let me say that no Churchman, liable to pay this just and legal due, has ever yet demurred to its payment and that I can hardly think that a Company which owns a Journal claiming to defend Constitutional principles and more especially the connection between Church and State, would wish to avail itself of my determination not to prosecute non-paying parishioners because there were some Dissenters who conscientiously could not see their way to pay. . . ."

If Mr. Pereira imagined that his line of attack would shame the Company into paying up, he was very much mistaken. The Manager was instructed to inform the reverend gentleman that, "in consequence of his not having acted fairly to this Company by taking his printing out of the parish, the directors did not feel justified in paying the dues and on that account the cheque had been withheld".

There is no further mention of Mr. Pereira's name in the records of the Company.

CHAPTER 4

Passmore Edwards

THE SHORT-LIVED attempt to publish an evening paper in
the year 1870 had aroused the scorn rather than the fears of the
board. Fifteen years later they felt very differently. In March,
1885, the directors placed on record their opinion that such a
newspaper should be launched by the Hampshire Advertiser
Company, if only to forestall a possible competitor. As a
preliminary, they sent Henry King to London to see a firm that
had offered to supply stereo type and to make other inquiries.
His report convinced them the matter was of so much importance that it would be best to consult the principal shareholders,
but for some reason nothing was done until the December. A
special board meeting, to which Messrs. R. S. Hankinson.
W. Gordon. G. P. Perkins, J. O. Parmenter and W. A.
Hankinson had been invited as representatives of the shareholders, then passed a resolution stating that "it is expedient to
publish and issue an Evening Newspaper for Southampton and
that the price of the same be one halfpenny".

The expediency of such a course had been made doubly
plain by the unwelcome news that the Hampshire Independent
Company had sold their paper and its printing plant to Mr.
Passmore Edwards. This could mean only one thing: the
millionaire philanthropist intended to start an evening paper in
Southampton in the Liberal interest.

Edwards was a remarkable man. A Cornishman born in
humble circumstances, he made a fortune in newspaper and
periodical publishing and spent his money generously,

endowing public libraries, hospitals, convalescent homes, art galleries, children's homes, drinking fountains, museums, technical institutes and orphanages. He supported most of the progressive movements of his day – free trade, pacifism, co-operation – and believed that education would "go far towards making bloodshed more and more distasteful to man, and thus do something towards establishing a brotherhood among peoples".

Like Lord Beaverbrook in our own times, he published newspapers chiefly in order to propagate his political and social ideas, and in doing so made a great deal of money. The enormous success of his *London Echo* – the first $\frac{1}{2}d$. evening paper to appear in Britain – sent him into the provinces looking for fresh fields to conquer. Since 1880 he had represented Salisbury in Parliament ("I found stimulation in the thought that the poor Cornish boy, after many buffetings with fortune, should represent a cathedral city"), and among the papers he controlled was the *Salisbury Times*. Of the *Southern Echo*, it was said that he conceived it and practically set it going in twenty-four hours. But we must not get ahead of time. At this point in the narrative the founding of the Southampton evening was still two or three years in the future.

But in 1885 other evening papers from outside Southampton were circulating in the district, and their competition was beginning to damage the old-established weeklies – particularly the *Hampshire Independent*, which had been going down hill for some time. At a board meeting of the Independent Company held on October 26 in that year, and attended by Henry Pinnoch, J.P. (Chairman), Alfred Pegler, J. J. Burnett and James Blach, the Secretary reported that not only had the paper's circulation suffered, but that the acceptance of small advertisements by the evening dailies at 6d. an insertion had reduced its revenue from the same source. On the other hand, expenses were increasing. The report continued thus: "We were at great expense in reporting Liberal county meetings without any corresponding result by way of advertisements, the Corrupt Practices Act restricting a candidate's expenditure in this direction. Of the outstanding accounts, the Southampton Liberal Association owed £102 3s. 6d. As to the direction in which expenses could be curtailed, he suggested it would be impossible to continue at its present basis the salary of the manager which, without solicitation, the directors had kindly increased from £200 to £250 a year, and that the reporting staff might be diminished when the election was over."

Such being the low state of the *Independent*'s fortunes, it is not surprising that its proprietors were glad to sell to Passmore Edwards when he made them a reasonable offer. On December 14, 1885, the paper's directors reported that a provisional agreement had been entered into with Mr. Edwards for the sale of the entire property of the company, subject to the approval of the shareholders at a meeting to be called as soon as practicable. There were no further entries in the minute book of the Independent Company, which had now passed into the possession of the Storey-Carnegie Syndicate, of which Passmore Edwards was the principal shareholder; that at least is the inference to be drawn from E. H. Burrage's biography *J. Passmore Edwards, Philanthropist*.[1] The directors of the Hampshire Advertiser Company continued to play with the idea of starting a daily, but as Passmore Edwards seemed to be in no hurry to do so, they saw no reason for haste. In the New Year of 1886 the Manager made another trip to Fleet Street for the purpose of discovering how much it would cost to run a journal of this kind, and he returned with discouraging news. His inquiries showed that at first there would be a loss of at least £500 a year, and that the "project altogether would be doubtful and risky".

Once again the matter was fully discussed by the directors, whose enthusiasm was now ebbing away. In the end they "were

---

[1] "The Storey-Carnegie Syndicate was formed for the promotion and publication of certain papers including the well-known (London) *Echo*. The *Hampshire Independent*, *Southern Echo* and *Salisbury Times* were among the publications produced under the guidance of Mr. Passmore Edwards, and it was said of the *Southern Echo* that he conceived it and practically set it going in twenty-four hours. His share in the group of papers was one-third. . . ."

inclined to think" that it would prove of greater advantage to the Company, and be more popular with the public, if the price of Saturday's edition of the *Advertiser* were reduced to 1d. (but this time without any guarantee from the Conservative Party!). It was decided to refer the whole question to a formal meeting of the shareholders.

The situation was dramatically changed when, on August 20, 1888, Passmore Edwards brought out the first issue of the *Southern Echo*. The Advertiser Company could not ignore this challenge. They must either produce an evening paper of their own or make a bid for the *Echo*, and after a few months they decided to adopt the latter course.

It seems that Passmore Edwards personally edited and managed the *Echo* in the first months of the paper's life. This was characteristic of the man, as we learn from his biographer: "Of the exacting nature of the work entailed by the production of a daily newspaper, only those who have had the experience can have the faintest idea. There must be unceasing watchfulness, untiring energy and sound judgment in selecting and arranging matter, if success is to be attained and, being attained, be preserved. One paper would of itself suffice to tax the mental and physical powers of most men, but to have to keep a watchful eye on several, noting defects, suggesting improvements and guiding members of the staff in the way they should go, is a labour few would undertake; or having undertaken it, very few are able to survive for long the wear and tear of the immense amount of labour entailed. Yet Mr. Passmore Edwards undertook the work and never turned from it or fainted by the way, for full thirty years".[1]

No less typical of the man was the way in which the *Echo* celebrated its arrival on the Southampton scene. Edwards, a benevolent, bearded figure, presided in person over a party given to the paper's newsboys – waifs and strays who depended for their living on the coppers they earned. "A very interesting sight", the paper reported, "was presented at the Victoria

[1] E. H. Burrage, *op. cit.*

Skating Rink, Southampton, when from 130 to 140 lads, many
of them shoeless, and probably as many fatherless, were
entertained by the proprietor of the *Southern Echo* to a meat tea,
followed by an entertainment." But Passmore Edwards did
not think that the social problem could be solved by giving
meat teas to hungry newsboys. He sent his reporters to
investigate the slum conditions of the courts and alleys behind
Southampton's High Street which we encountered earlier in
this history. He also gave space in his columns to the legitimate
grievances of the poor and unemployed, attacked abuses and
campaigned for improvements. He was in fact a crusading
owner-editor.

An article which must have caused a stir in the town began
like this: "It is a shock to find that Southampton furnishes
sights and scenes of bitter, grinding poverty, keen and unendurable as those painted by Mr. Sims in *How the Poor Live* or those
revealed in the pages of the Factory Inspector's Report. . . ."
The *Echo* investigator, walking from Western Shore (not yet
industrialised) to High Street, found "densely-peopled, evil-
smelling, close courts". Windows were broken and stuffed
with rags. Doors hung awry. In the gutters ill-clad children
were playing, and everywhere drunkenness, vice and disease
were "painfully evident".

It was in this year 1888 that the Gordon Boys' Brigade was
founded in Southampton. Reporting this event, the *Echo*
recalled that "one of the most interesting chapters in the biography of our great fellow townsman, General C. G. Gordon"
was that which related to his care for the ragged urchins of
Gravesend: his "Scutlers" and his "Kings". "His concern for
them", the writer continued, "did not cease when they left
him for the Army or the Navy or business, and his thoughts and
prayers followed them wherever they went. It is particularly
fitting therefore that the recently established organisation in
Southampton for the purpose of finding employment for
deserving lads should bear his honoured name." The Brigade
consisted of sixty boys, most of them orphans, who were

provided with "neat, smart uniforms of blue serge, faced with scarlet". (Gordon, by the way, had been dead four years when the Brigade bearing his name was founded. He was universally regarded as a martyr-hero, and the *Advertiser* agreed with Queen Victoria in holding Mr. Gladstone and his Liberal Government, rather than the Mahdi, responsible for his untimely end!)

In those early pages of the *Echo* we can detect not only the political and social ideals of Passmore Edwards but also his cultural interests. John Ruskin, then the dictator of artistic taste, was reported as saying that the National Gallery in London was now "the most important collection of paintings in Europe for the general student". General Pitt-Rivers, founder of the modern British school of archaeology, was one of the star speakers at that year's meeting of the British Association for the Advancement of Science, and his subject was prehistoric man in Wiltshire. In Glasgow, we learn, Henry Irving was appearing in *Faust*. The most-discussed novelist of the day was Zola, and the *Echo* printed an interview with him on the subject of marriage. The wily Frenchman did not commit himself.

Sport, as one would expect, figured prominently in the new evening paper. The Australian XI was then touring the country, but did not command the biggest headlines in those days. What was causing quite a stir, however, was the growth of women's cricket. Then, as now, means of locomotion made good copy, and the first issues of the *Echo* contained several critical paragraphs about the railways. In the Isle of Wight there were too many, and none seemed to be paying a dividend. But on the mainland – in Hampshire at least – there were still too few, and the Didcot, Newbury and Southampton Railway (with whose shortcomings we are already familiar) was taken to task for not having continued its line from Winchester to Southampton. The *Echo* reported with approval that more passengers travelled first class on the London and South Western Railway than on any other, but showed hostility to second-class carriages, which, it said, were "slowly but steadily disappearing". Demands – still unheeded in the 1960s – were being made for a fast service between Bristol and the South Coast.

That year the Union Line steamer *Tartar* set up a new world record by completing the voyage from the Cape to Plymouth (then Southampton's great rival) in seventeen days, fifty-nine minutes. (In 1938 the *Carnarvon Castle* made the journey in twelve days, thirteen hours, thirty-eight minutes.) In the Isle of Wight they were thinking about starting electric trams (but they never did), and in Southampton the horse-drawn kind were earning their shareholders a modest $2\frac{1}{2}$ per cent. dividend. But the most exciting items in this class of news dealt not with ships or trains, but with aviation. The sky, you would think, was full of balloons. The sight of one floating above St. Paul's Cathedral held up traffic in the City. They crossed the Channel; they got lost in the mountains of the North; and one day in 1888 a balloon navigated by Simmonds, the greatest aviator of the time, crashed, and its "pilot" was killed. An *Echo* reporter, who knew him well and had been up with him, wrote his obituary.

All this represented something new in local journalism. The crusading spirit, the bright, descriptive writing, the snappy paragraphs and the human-interest stories must have appealed to many who were bored by the old-established weeklies with their close-set columns about local and national politics. But, of course, politics did fill quite a lot of space in the *Echo* of seventy-six years ago. The sensation of the moment was the Parnell Case, and when Gladstone, formidable in Opposition, came out strongly in defence of the libelled Irish Nationalist, the *Echo* approved. In a leader it growled:

"Fair play is claimed as a characteristic of Englishmen, and

---

1 J. H. Goldsmith (General Manager, 1910-24); 2 C. F. Carr (General Manager, 1948-57); 3 E. G. Burnett (Secretary, 1906-41); 4 H. J. Cheverton (Manager, *Bournemouth Daily Echo*, 1910-32); 5 R. Fairbairn (Manager, *Bournemouth Daily Echo*, 1932-53); 6 H. R. E. Baker (Advertisement Manager-in-chief, 1948-61); 7 G. Stephens (Manager, *Dorset Daily Echo*, 1921-9); 8 P. H. Thompson (Manager, *Dorset Daily Echo*, 1929-59); 9 E. J. Levi (London Manager, 1900-43); 10 W. A. Park (Editor, *Bournemouth Daily Echo*, 1900-47); 11 W. H. Hill (Editor, *Dorset Daily Echo*, 1929-55); 12 F. George (Advertisement Manager, *Southern Daily Echo*; died 1938).

EXECUTIVES AND HEADS OF DEPARTMENTS, SOUTHAMPTON

Front row: Messrs. G. Baker (Accountant), F. H. Mills (Mechanical Superintendent), Rodney Andrew, J.P. (Deputy General Manager and Editor of *Southern Evening Echo*), R. R. Gleave, O.B.E., J.P. (Director and General Manager), G. W. O'Connor (Assistant Manager and Assistant Editor), H. F. S. Kimber (Advertisement Manager-in-chief), M. Stone (Assistant Secretary).

Centre row: Messrs. S. A. Russell (Stereo Overseer), S. Weyman (Process Overseer), Gordon Sewell (Chief Leader-Writer), A. E. Rawlings (Sports Editor), P. D. Treseder (Executive Assistant), L. Cross (Circulation Manager), R. Fray (Cashier), J. W. Macdonald (Publisher), P. Raynes (Chief Librarian).

Rear row: Messrs. W. Cole (Transport Manager), G. F. Crane (Assistant Advertisement Manager), A. L. Smith (News Editor), B. J. Hall (Chief Sub-Editor), E. O. E. Wickes (Chief Telegraphist), J. H. Adams (Chief Photographer), G. Bryer (Advertisement Promotion Manager), A. F. Steward

EXECUTIVES AND HEADS OF DEPARTMENTS, BOURNEMOUTH

Front row: Messrs. R. A. S. Coles (Composing Room Overseer), G. F. King (Chief Sub-Editor), E. J. V. Guppy (Chief Cashier), D. H. Sims (Editor), D. A. Gleave (Manager), S. Carey (Assistant Manager), H. A. Wills (Chief Accountant), C. W. J. Marsh (Process Manager), G. H. Kennett (Press Room Overseer).

Back row: Messrs. E. C. G. Mesher (Transport Manager), A. C. Polden (Publisher), K. F. Austin (Chief Process Engraver), H. C. Skinner (Chief Stereotyper), E. D. Kemp (Chief Telegraphist), R. W. Harrison (Sports Editor), W. G. Young (Chief Reporter), L. Wherrett (Chief Advertisement Representative), H. W. Ashley (Chief Photographer).

EXECUTIVES AND HEADS OF DEPARTMENTS, WEYMOUTH

Front row: C. B. Randall (Chief Sub-Editor), A. R. Adlam, J.P. (Editor), A. B. Burnett (Manager), W. S. Handle (Advertisement Manager), R. M. Wickett (Chief Reporter).

Back row: L. C. Spring (News-Room Overseer), A. H. Ellis (Accountant), G. Roper (Chief Driver), D. Butler (Publisher), H. Babb (Chief Tele-printer Operator), S. H. Williams (Press-Room Overseer) if it is so Mr. Parnell has been handicapped in an unEnglish fashion by the Ministers of the Crown . . . Justice is not infallible in its discrimination and relies too often on the guiding hand of well-fed counsel to arrive at a decision. The man with a long purse is, in consequence, a formidable enemy to fight, even in a righteous cause, and Mr. Gladstone in clear and emphatic language indicated the danger Mr. Parnell runs in his battle with the wealthy *Times* before the Special Commission. . . ."

Commenting on another speech of Gladstone's at this time – his denunciation of the treatment of political prisoners in Ireland – the *Echo* remarked that people who were "stirred to the depths by Russian punishment of Nihilist assassins or by King Bomba's method of dealing with Neopolitan conspirators", defended the punishment of Irishmen, whose only offence was a political one, as if they were "vile and brutalised criminals".

There were frequent news stories about repression in Russia, and attention was often drawn to the poverty of the *moujiks*. But Russia was not at that time regarded as a danger to peace. The *Echo* at any rate was more concerned about the intentions of Germany. It reported keen German competition in trade and in the race for African colonies, and cited as evidence of the Kaiser's warlike disposition his fondness for the *Kriegspiel*.

Returning to local affairs, we find the *Echo* informing its readers that the Southampton School Board intended to spend £3,600 on public education in the year ending March, 1889, and deploring the fact that the town possessed no public library – a subject near to Passmore Edwards' heart. In spite of the trade depression, the docks were doing well, the tonnage using the port in the previous year having amounted to 1,092,172 (about a twentieth of the annual average in the 1960s).

Overshadowing all these events were the Jack the Ripper murders in Whitechapel. Day after day in the latter months of 1888 these held the *Echo* headline.

The times were stirring, and the new evening paper matched the times. The gentlemen in the *Advertiser* board room were concerned about their rival's successful debut.

D

CHAPTER 5

Buying the Echo

THE KEEN WIND of competition was blowing through the newspaper offices of Southampton in the autumn of 1888, and it disturbed a few cobwebs in the editorial department of the *Hampshire Advertiser.* At a meeting of the directors in the September – a month after the *Echo* had been launched – the following resolution was adopted: "That, looking to the severe competition of the present time and the requirements of the public in the direction of vigorous and spirited writing, the directors – after much deliberation – have reluctantly come to the conclusion that a change in the editorship of the paper is absolutely necessary. They have therefore with much regret to convey to Mr. Collett a request that he will send in his resignation as Editor of the paper."

Collett had twenty-seven years' service to his credit and had apparently always given satisfaction in the past. It was the bright new journalism of Passmore Edwards' *Echo* that had caused the board to look with a more critical eye at the old-fashioned treatment of news and politics in the columns of the *Hampshire Advertiser.* But although they were determined on a change in the editorship, they were not without sympathy for the man who had served them for so long, and when Collett asked that he might continue as assistant editor at a reduced salary, if the leading articles were supplied by "a more skilled hand", they agreed to retain his services and advertise for a leader-writer.

In December of that memorable year a meeting of the board

was called for the express purpose of considering the advisability of treating for the purchase of the *Hampshire Independent*
and the *Southern Echo*. Passmore Edwards had asked Lord
Wolmer £15,000 for the two papers, but Henry King under-
stood that he was now willing to sell for £12,000. Lord
Wolmer was apparently no longer interested on his own
account, but might act as an intermediary – so the Manager was
instructed to see him and ask him to write to Mr. Edwards and
"request him to name the very lowest price he was prepared to
take for the business".

Nothing seems to have come of Lord Wolmer's good offices,
for in the following January we find the board resolving to
negotiate direct with Mr. Passmore Edwards and arranging for
the Manager to "wait upon that gentleman and ascertain if he
was disposed to sell the company and at what price".

The negotiations thus begun were to continue for over two
years before being brought to a successful conclusion; it was
not until April, 1891, that the Common Seal of the Hampshire
Advertiser Company was attached to the preliminary agreement for the purchase of the *Southern Echo* and the *Hampshire
Independent*.

Henry King's first encounter with Passmore Edwards took
place in London immediately after the board meeting at which
he had been instructed to open negotiations. On this occasion
the newspaper magnate seems to have done most of the talking.
With a great show of frankness, he told the emissary from
Southampton exactly how much he had paid for the Independent Company: £10,000 for the copyright and goodwill of the
newspaper and £1,200 for the machinery and plant of the
short-lived *Evening Star*. In addition he had spent £500 on
alterations to the premises, and some hundreds on launching the
Southern Echo.

"I am prepared to take £12,000 for the whole concern, less
the book debts," he told King.

But the Manager formed the opinion that Passmore Edwards
would in fact be prepared to take a much lower price if one

were firmly offered, and that is what he told the board when he reported back.

Edwards had made it plain that he expected the Advertiser Company to make him an offer, but the directors were in no hurry to commit themselves. The trouble was that in buying the *Echo* they would also be acquiring their old rival, the *Hampshire Independent*. Would it not be an embarrassment for a firm of Conservative newspaper publishers to be responsible for the conduct of a Liberal journal? But who would take the *Independent*, with its falling circulation, off their hands? Before coming to any further decision they resolved to find out whether its Managing Editor, Mr. Henry Lashmore, might be interested in persuading a few of his wealthier Liberal friends to subscribe and float a public company for carrying on the paper in the Radical interest.

Nothing came of this, and for eighteen months negotiations seem to have been in suspense. The next we hear of the project to buy the *Echo* is at a board meeting in July, 1890, when the Manager reported that he had seen Passmore Edwards, who had offered to sell the *Independent* and the *Southern Echo* for the same price that he had paid. Again the directors hesitated. They agreed that it was important that the papers should be acquired, but they were still uncertain about how much they should pay for them. So once more Henry King was packed off to London on a one-man fact-finding mission. His instructions were "to obtain from Mr. Edwards some figures showing the income, book debts, value of premises, etc." But the latter could not easily be pinned down to such details, and when King next faced his directors – in August – the only definite information he was able to give them was that the *Echo* and the *Independent* could be had for £10,000 with book debts, but this sum would not include the job-printing business or the premises. "With regard to getting some idea of the profits and information as to book debts, value of premises, etc., Mr. Edwards said he would shortly be in Southampton and would call to see Mr. King."

Passmore Edwards did not keep his promise, and by November Henry King was beginning to feel anxious about what the outcome of the whole affair might be. He told the board that the *Echo* was making great headway and that he thought "something should be done". The directors agreed with him, but what *could* be done until some way had been found of disposing of the *Independent*? After a long discussion, it was decided that King should approach an agent in London "with a view to trying to sell the *Independent* or to starting a company to carry it on". The Manager was also instructed to see Passmore Edwards again.

A new and more hopeful turn in events occurred after King had made the acquaintance of Walter Wellsman, of the London firm of Mitchell & Company, newspaper valuers. The expert was optimistic. He thought he knew "two or three gentlemen" who would be interested in buying the *Independent*, but pointed out that it would be useless to approach them without definite figures.

This was obviously the man the board had been looking for. In future, they decided, he should act as their intermediary, and they would pay him his expenses while the negotiations were being conducted, and the usual commission when they were satisfactorily completed. To begin with, he would see Mr. Edwards on their behalf and obtain from him figures showing what the concern had been doing, and get permission to inspect the plant and report on its probable value.

The valuer's report throws such an interesting light on provincial newspaper production seventy odd years ago that it should be read in full:

"January, 1891.

"In accordance with your instructions, I visited the *Hampshire Independent* and *Southern Echo* offices on Saturday last with an introduction from Mr. Passmore Edwards. I inspected the plant of the daily paper and found it in excellent order, very complete, exceedingly clean and evidently ample for the purpose. The Victory, though an old one, is well kept, and so far as I could ascertain from the engineer does its work fairly well; it is driven by an 8-horse gas engine, also in good condition. The stereo apparatus also appears to be in good order. I find that the two-feeder Wharfedale used for the *Independent* does its work well, and to drive it and for other purposes they have a $3\frac{1}{2}$-horse gas engine. The entire plant of the newspaper office is on one floor with plenty of room for development if necessary. There are various presses and machines ample for all ordinary purposes.

"The jobbing plant in the room above is one of the most complete I have seen in a Country Newspaper Office; it is equal to any ordinary emergency and the stock of fancy and wood letter is unusually full.

"Having gone through the office, Mr. F. Edwards told me that they employed about 45 people for the production of the two papers and the jobbing work. He was not instructed to give me any information as to the amount of profit derived from the paper, and I gathered from him that the turnover of the whole business was about £9,000 per annum, and that the book debts generally might be said to be £3,000. I asked him as to the circulation of the *Independent* and whether it had suffered at all from the *Echo* being published. He told me, no; that on the contrary the circulation had increased for 1890. Questioned as to the position the *Echo* occupied, he tacitly admitted that it was not making a profit. He told me it was fairly on the way, that all the advertisements in it, both 'situations' and others, were *bona fide*, and that no fill-ups appeared in its pages.

"Looking to the whole matter as a going concern, I am strongly of the opinion that it would be a very good purchase for the Company to make. I admit that the price is high. But in the peculiar circumstances under which it is proposed to be taken, it would be absolutely necessary to pay somewhat more than the market values. I have been in negotiation with a

gentleman who might perhaps be disposed to take over the
Independent. . . .

Walter Wellsman,
Licensed valuer, 15.1.91."

An encouraging report – but still no statement of profit and
loss! Wellsman was asked to have another "go" at Passmore
Edwards about this, but the latter declined to say what the
profit or loss had been or what the expenses of management
were. He simply repeated that, since he had not provided any
money for the carrying on of the papers, they must have been
paying their way.

At this point in the negotiations the *Advertiser* directors were
receiving advice from several quarters. First there was Mr.
Jeans, the London representative of the *Dundee Courier* and the
Leeds Mercury, who was prepared to purchase the *Independent,*
"provided he found everything to be as represented after he had
inspected the books and premises". Next there was Mr. Bland,
one of the proprietors of the *Gloucester Citizen,* who gave Mr.
King important information respecting the working of an
evening newspaper. And, finally, Mr. Marchmont of Preston,
who had had considerable experience of evening newspaper
work and who went most fully into the subject.

Better informed than ever, the directors now felt in a position
to make Passmore Edwards a firm offer. They were willing to
pay him £10,000 for the whole concern, but only £2,000 in
cash; the remaining £8,000 was to remain on mortgage at, say,
4 per cent., the Company giving as security the first charge on
the *Independent* and *Echo* copyrights, premises and plant.
Edwards flatly declined, and when the board met again – on
March 26, 1891 – the Manager confessed that he had failed to
reach agreement with the proprietor of the *Echo,* whose latest
terms were £8,000 in cash or £12,000 with half the sum owed
remaining on mortgage for three or five years at 5 per cent.

Taking Edwards at his word, the board replied with an offer
of £8,000 in cash for the *Independent* and *Echo* copyrights,

plant, jobbing business and premises – the book debts at a valuation. This met with yet another refusal, Passmore Edwards now saying that he must have the full amount the undertaking had cost him. Would the Advertiser Company be willing to pay him £9,500 at once and an additional £2,500 out of the book debts when these had been collected?

By way of reply the board sent off the following telegram: "DIRECTORS NOW SITTING RESOLVED TO MAKE YOU ONE MORE OFFER STOP £8,500 IN CASH BOOK DEBTS AS YOU SUGGESTED."

When they met ten days later, on April 16, the following reply from Passmore Edwards was read out to them: "OFFER RESPECTFULLY DECLINED". It looked like stalemate. All we can learn from the record is that the meeting, having discussed the subject, broke up without deciding on any further action being taken.

The impasse did not last long, however. On April 24 Henry King reported that he had been instructed by the directors individually to see Mr. Passmore Edwards and had arranged with him the terms of purchase of the *Hampshire Independent* and the *Southern Echo* as follows: "We give him £9,500 for the *Hants Independent* and *Southern Echo* copyrights, job-printing business (subject to mortgage of £3,000) and prefer-ence shares in the Swindon Marlborough Railway Company. As to book debts, we are to collect same on Mr. Edwards's behalf and be paid compensation for so doing at 5 per cent. After £2,500 has been collected we are entitled to the re-mainder . . . £500 deposit to be paid and the balance on completion of the purchase, say June 1 next."

So at last it looked as though these long-drawn-out negotia-tions – which had sometimes seemed more like the haggling which takes place in Oriental bazaars! – were about to reach their end. Mr. Edwards had written accepting these terms, and a draft agreement drawn by the Advertiser Company's lawyers, Messrs. Lomer & Son, was read to the board and approved, clause by clause. The bank, it appeared, would advance the necessary funds for the purchase, provided the

Company would grant them debentures for the amount. Five days later the Common Seal of the Company was attached to this preliminary agreement.

Having brought this important affair to a successful conclusion, the directors now turned their attention to another threat of serious competition. It had come to their knowledge that "several Conservative gentlemen in the town were about to buy the *Observer* and publish it at 1*d.* in the Conservative interest" and that they had been promised financial backing. Clearly this constituted a threat to the Tory *Advertiser*, which was still being published at 2*d.*, and if necessary the board was prepared to buy out the *Observer*.

Henry King was sent to establish contact with the "enemy", and he returned with a reassuring reconnaissance report. The promoters of the *Observer* scheme expected to receive an offer from the Advertiser Company, but now that the *Advertiser* had bought the *Echo* and intended issuing it daily, the necessity for publishing the *Observer* at 1*d.* was done away with. They would be prepared to sell the paper to the *Advertiser* at cost price plus legal expenses.

The board was no longer interested, and the matter was dropped.

At a meeting of shareholders on May 28, 1891, the directors were authorised to borrow £20,000 on debentures.

The last issue of the *Echo* to bear the imprint "Published by F. A. Edwards for the Proprietor" appeared on July 14, 1891. On the following day the wording was changed to "Published by H. King for the Proprietors". The address remained the same: 52 Above Bar, Southampton, the premises from which the *Independent* had been published for many years. On this site (since re-numbered) stands the present headquarters of Southern Newspapers Limited.

CHAPTER 6

Town and Port

HERE WE MUST pause to take note of one of the most important events in the history of Southampton during the second half of the nineteenth century. On July 26, 1890, the ageing Queen Victoria crossed from Osborne, her island retreat, to the mainland in her yacht, the *Victoria and Albert*, for the purpose of opening the Empress Dock.

Probably no news story had previously been given such extensive coverage by the local Press. The *Advertiser* and the *Independent* each devoted a page to the ceremony and the history of the docks. The *Echo* (still under the command of Passmore Edwards) carried fourteen close-set columns and an artist's impression of the docks viewed from the air. The special article appearing in its companion paper, the *Independent*, it announced, had been prepared in book form and neatly bound, and had been forwarded in advance to Her Majesty the Queen "in the hope that the history and description there given would be of some interest in view of today's proceedings". In acknowledging this presentation copy, the Queen's Secretary, Sir Henry Ponsonby, referred by name to the current holder of the *Independent* editorship – a Mr. Stentiford.

From the issue of the *Hampshire Advertiser* of July 26 we learn that "the new Empress Dock which is now to be inaugurated has been a source of considerable anxiety to the Dock Company during its construction, owing to the exceptional difficulties their engineer and the contractors have had to contend against in the treacherous foundation of peat which formed the dock bottom. This was the cause of a sudden subsidence of the north-west wall, which delayed the completion of the work".

This might be irreverently described as the Dock Company's last fling. Already the London and South Western Railway Company was negotiating for the purchase of the enterprise, and – the necessary legislation having been passed into law – it took charge of the Docks on November 1, 1892.

The town and the railway, which had so often been at loggerheads, were now well and truly reconciled. As the writer of a special article remarked in the *Echo* of October 29, "There have been many fights in the past between our local legislators and the South Western Railway Company, but the enlightened and far-seeing policy of Mr. C. Scotter, the General Manager, backed up by an able board of directors, has done away with all friction. The most friendly relations between the Town and the Company now exist, and there can be no doubt that the success of the Docks must mean the increased prosperity of the port."

Mr. John Dixon, newly appointed by the railway as its Docks Superintendent, told a local gathering that some people imagined that he had come to make Southampton the Liverpool of the South, but he assured them he had no such intention. "Southampton was going to be Southampton without comparison, invidious or otherwise. Southampton was bound to be *the* ocean port of England. . . . There is at the present time an immense competition for ocean traffic, and the port offering the best facilities will be the most successful. And can any port offer better – nay, equal – facilities to Southampton, when its great undertaking has been properly and thoroughly developed?"

The implied promise of development was soon put into effect, and three years later, on August 3, 1895, the Prince of Wales came to Southampton to open the world's largest graving dock. As the *Echo* put it: "When the South Western Company acquired the Docks they at once realised the fact that if they wished to extend the commerce of the port they must have adequate provision for the ocean greyhounds which they invited to the place. With characteristic energy and enterprise, the Company determined to construct the largest graving dock in the world." This, in the *Echo*'s opinion, was one more step towards attaining "supremacy in maritime affairs". (The editorial went on to recall that the Prince and Princess of Wales had visited Southampton on their wedding day, when they were received by Sir Frederick Perkins as Mayor at a "gorgeous" reception in "splendid" surroundings.)

We talk of the Gay Nineties without perhaps any real justification. But there was at least one day in that decade when the whole nation rejoiced and made holiday – the Diamond Jubilee of the Queen's Accession, in 1897. It was a day marked by civic, religious and military ceremonials, but the formal celebrations were less important than the spontaneous expressions of joy and loyalty from the Queen's subjects in every class and walk of life. This aspect of the Jubilee was caught by an *Echo* reporter who mingled with the immense crowds which filled Southampton's main thoroughfares on that memorable night:

"As soon as the sun began to sink into the west the people began to flock back to town, and the streets soon became absolutely impassable. The crush was particularly noticeable in the vicinity of the Bargate, and even the police were now and again completely nonplussed. Mounted constabulary backed their horses into the crowd, and did not get unmixed thanks for this simple endeavour to do their duty. Heavily laden trams were blocked at every few yards, whilst an interminable string of cabs caused no little discomfort to the thousands of pedestrians who thronged the streets. It was a swinging, swaying but, on the whole, good-tempered crowd, and probably never in the history of the town has there been such a concourse of people in the streets. The effect produced by the multicoloured lights, casting as they did their luminous rays on the variegated bunting, which the evening breeze lazily stirred, was grand in the extreme. And as the several establishments, whose illuminating power was supplied by electricity, leaped instantaneously into light, the effect produced was at once charming and novel."

In its leading article the *Echo* gave a classic expression to the self-confidence of Victorian England at the height of her power and influence:

"India and our Colonies had sent us their sons to lead the Queen in her march of celebration. . . . Politicians came as patriots from the Colonies to our parade of thanksgiving. They were at the centre of movement, the great throbbing heart of our civilisation. They had come home, descendants of the men and women who went out as humble emigrants, to cast happy eyes on the land of their fathers, to be honoured as part and parcel of the Empire. The dark-skinned men who were not united to us by race or religion were warmly welcomed. . . . They must have felt it no humiliation to be attached to such a vigorous, teeming people, whose sons traverse the world. Our American cousins must have been glad of their kinship, and looking forward to the time when the English-speaking race shall dominate the earth. Strangers and pilgrims from other lands must have caught some quicker insight into the greatness of the British people, the affection with which the Queen is regarded, the vitality which has compelled us to explore, to colonise, and to build up free States afar off.

"It is Geffcken", the leader continued, quoting a forgotten German historian, "who has voiced the idea that will affect them when he says: 'Nowhere in history do we find an example of a State which on the map of the world occupies so small a space, ruling, at a distance so great, an empire so large.' It is only as we realise this ourselves that we shall understand the meaning of Jubilee Day, catch the full glory of the sixty years of history now completed, and be able to read aright the simple words, 'God save the Queen'."

After so much noble rhetoric, it is perhaps a relief to read an *Echo* news item which states that ambulance nurses had told a reporter that tight-lacing was responsible for most of the cases of fainting among women which they had treated during the Jubilee holiday!

The leader-writer had written as though the whole Colonial Empire were united in fervent loyalty to Victoria's Crown. He had, understandably in the circumstances, omitted to mention the Boers, who, unlike the dark-skinned Indians, did regard it as a humiliation to be subjected to British rule. Hardly had the tumult and the cheering of the Jubilee died away than the first shots were being fired in the South African War, which broke out in 1899. It was a long time since England had been involved in a serious conflict, and that was probably why this break in civilian routine was welcomed by many with almost hysterical enthusiasm. But as the war dragged on ("We shall muddle through," said Lord Milner) the mood of the public changed.

Southampton, perhaps, was unable to view the war in an objective fashion. After all, this was the great chance for which the port had been waiting all through the century. The modern facilities provided by the docks had enabled the War Office to embark an army in record time, and the townspeople enjoyed basking in reflected glory. Mr. Owens, an official from Waterloo, summed up the port's achievement when he told the members of the Chamber of Commerce, dining amid the baroque splendours of the new South-Western Hotel, that "never in the history of Southampton had its facilities and advantages loomed so high in the eyes of the whole world". When the final count came to be taken at the end of the war, the figures were certainly impressive. Nearly half a million troops, with their equipment, horses and munitions of war, passed through the port. No wonder there were addresses of welcome for Earl Roberts and Sir Redvers Buller when they returned from South Africa in November, 1900. These were boom days for Southampton.

Here is an article typical of many which appeared in the *Echo* at that time:

"Oh! the glory of it! Oh, the pathos and sorrow! Within the past few weeks thousands of persons have visited

Southampton to see the embarkation of the troops, to whom the honour and success of this Empire are entrusted. . . . There are three classes of men going out to the war: first there are the young and unmarried, who have none dependent upon them, and who can look on the coming conflict with light, nay, with pleasurable anticipations to seeing what a battlefield really is. Then you have the married men who are bidding goodbye to wives and children; who proudly point to the service they hope to render their Queen and country; who assure the 'missus' that the parting is only for a time, and who keep up a brave spirit throughout. And, last, you have the reservist; the man who, since he left the ranks, has lived at home in peace and quietude; who has been bringing up his family in a manner highly respectable, yet who is suddenly summoned to rejoin the colours. And though he does so with every heartiness and good-will, what a wrench thus to be taken from home, and all that is near and dear. . . . Not merely Southampton, or indeed England, is watching the Docks today. The world looks on and realises that the serious moment is at hand, and that the struggle will shortly commence in dead earnest."

When the news flashed around the world that Mafeking had been relieved, Southampton went mad with the rest of England. "The paroxysm of excitement and enthusiasm with which the town was seized on Saturday", reported the *Echo* on May 21, 1900, "reached its wildest degree in the evening, when a torchlight procession paraded the principal thorough-fares in the sight of cheering thousands." There were no elaborate preparations, but this didn't matter, said the *Echo*, because "patriotism, spontaneous and splendid, saw that the procession achieved its purpose".

We read that the cheering was so loud at times that it could have been heard miles away. Rarely if ever had such a scene been witnessed in Southampton, "but while intoxicated with excitement and enthusiasm, the crowds were splendidly be-haved and gave not the least trouble to the police . . .". The climax to the evening came when "Oom Paul's" effigy was consigned to the flames amid the jeers and groans of the crowd. "As far as Southampton is concerned", commented the *Echo*, "all that remains of President Kruger is a charred piece of wood, which might be found in some gutter near the Free Library."

Not many months were to pass before the public mood was to undergo another abrupt transition: on January 22, 1901, the Victorian Age ended with the death of the great Queen at Osborne, her favourite residence, and the grief of the English people was expressed by Alfred Austin, the Poet Laureate, in a poem which the Echo published:

> *Dead! O the world feels widowed!*
> > *Can it be*
> *That she who scarce but yesterday upheld*
> *The dome of Empire, so the twain seemed one,*
> *Whose goodness shone and radiated round*
> *The circle of her still expanding Rule*
> *Whose sceptre was self-sacrifice, whose Throne*
> *Only a loftier height from which to scan*
> *The purpose of her People, their desires,*
> *Thoughts, hopes, fears, needs, joys, sorrows, sadnesses,*
> *Their strength in weal, their comforter in woe –*
> *That this her mortal habitation should*
> *Lie cold and tenantless! Alas! Alas!*

A whole page of the *Echo* was given over to the obituary of the Queen, and in a leader the paper declared that "good Queen Victoria is the best Sovereign this country has ever had, and if we grieve it is not without feeling the sweet satisfaction of having lived in her time".

The Hampshire Advertiser Company had existed for thirty-seven of the sixty-four years of the Victorian Age, and was now poised for a plunge into the twentieth century. It is time to return to its records.

Above: The first *Echo* office in Above Bar (1888).

Right: The second office, opened in 1906.

Above: The head office of the company in Above Bar, Southampton, as it looked in 1939 on the eve of the war.

Opposite: The same building after the air-raids of November 30–December 1, 1940. Passing the office is H.M. King George VI, accompanied by members of Southampton Corporation and the Government.

The present headquarters of Southern Newspapers Limited in Above Bar, Southampton.

CHAPTER 7

The Titanic *Era*

AT FIRST IT had seemed that the purchase of Passmore
Edwards' undertaking would depend upon the Hampshire
Advertiser Company being able to find a buyer for the
Independent. For, as we have noted, there was a reluctance on the
part of the *Advertiser* directors to be responsible for the running
of their old political rival. But although many inquiries were
received, the negotiations for the sale of the Liberal weekly
were unsuccessful. In the summer of 1891, just when the final
arrangements were being made for taking over the *Echo*,
Mr. Jeans, the London representative of the *Dundee Courier*
and the *Leeds Mercury*, offered £3,000 for the copyright and
goodwill of the *Independent*, together with the commercial
printing business. It is not clear whether he was acting on his
own behalf or as the agent of others, but in any case his offer
failed to interest the board. They wanted £4,000 for copyright
and goodwill and another £2,700 for the printing plant. The
equity of the premises they fixed at £2,000. Mr. Wellsman
"did not see his way clear to recommend his client to purchase
at the price asked", but if the directors would accept £3,900
for the goodwill and copyright he would try again.

Among others who made offers for the *Independent* in the
early 90s were W. Crosby Coles, W. B. Blackwell of Croydon,
and a Mr. Jennings of London. Crosby Coles, not unreasonably, asked for a valuation, but for some reason this was
refused. Jennings, however, was told that "the purchase of the
Independent must be effected on the basis of a lump sum, but the

directors would have no objection to his having a valuer go
through the plant for the purpose of furnishing him with
information for his own private use".

Nothing further is heard of the *Independent* being in the
market, and in fact the Company continued to publish their
former competitor until 1923, when it was amalgamated with
the *Hampshire Advertiser*.

At this time the directors were annoyed by the cool attitude
of the local Conservative authorities towards the *Hampshire
Advertiser*. It will be recalled that once the Tory chiefs had
valued the paper so highly that they had pressed the Company
to reduce the price in order that it might make a greater appeal
to the working classes. But in 1893, it seems, they no longer
recognised it as an official Conservative journal, or at least no
longer treated it as such. The board deputed one of its number,
Mr. Harper, to take this up with Colonel Crichton, a leading
local Conservative, but there is no record of his having been
successful. (In the previous year, when a wealthy group of
Conservatives had toyed with the idea of buying the *Independent* and running it as a Tory Party journal, Mr. Walter Perkins,
the Company's new Chairman, had taken the opportunity of
"speaking rather strongly to Lord Montagu of Beaulieu on the
way the Conservative Party had treated the *Advertiser*".)

In time the Company was to adopt a strictly independent,
non-party policy for all its journals, but no such decision had
yet been made. Indeed, the *Advertiser* was still describing itself
as a "Constitutional journal" in 1911 when, at last, it was able
to announce that its price had been reduced to 1*d.*:

"We very heartily wish all our readers a Happy and Prosperous New Year, and hope they will appreciate the progressive
policy which places from today a high-class, up-to-date
Constitutional journal within the reach of every Conservative
working man. In reducing the *Hampshire Advertiser* to a penny,
we are merely following out a policy to which we have
conscientiously adhered for no less a period than 88 years.
During all this time we have never wavered in our support of

the Conservative cause; but nevertheless it has been our earnest endeavour to keep abreast of the times, and it is in order to continue in that course that we publish the *Advertiser* at a penny today.... Conservative convictions are no longer the exclusive property of the wealthy classes. The loyal and patriotic masses who toil for their daily bread are the real backbone of the party, and it is with great pleasure that we now place a progressive penny paper advocating their own political views within their reach."

To go back to that memorable year, 1891, we find that in the August Henry King was able to inform the board that he had successfully concluded a new wages agreement with the compositors of the *Independent* and the *Echo*. On the same occasion the directors showed their appreciation of their Manager by increasing his salary to £400 a year, and their interest in club football by presenting an *Echo* Challenge Trophy worth £25. ("It will be a splendid advertisement for the paper," said Henry King, and the directors agreed.)

At first the *Echo* was run at a loss, but the steady increase in circulation and advertisements left little doubt in the minds of the directors that their newly-acquired property would soon begin to yield a profit. In those days even modest economies loomed large in the eyes of the board, however. Take, for example, the telephone contract. At the board meeting in March, 1892, the Manager reported that Mr. Edwards was under agreement with the Telephone Company to pay them £12 per annum for six years, four of which were unexpired. "The Company," he continued, "wish us to take over Mr. Edwards' liability, but a few months ago they offered to put the telephone into the *Advertiser* office for £6 5s. 6d. per annum. What is to be done?"

Mr. King was instructed to open negotiations with the telephone people and get the best possible terms, and as a result the old agreement was cancelled and a new one was entered into with the Hampshire Advertiser Company for four years at £6 13s. a year. The *Echo* was among the earliest subscribers of the Western Counties Telephone Company, which had opened an exchange in Southampton in 1888, the year in which the evening paper was founded. The Chamber of Commerce urged its members to use the new means of communication, and announced that its Honorary Secretary could supply pocket cards containing lists of subscribers!

Although few could have realised the fact at the time, the age of electricity had begun . . . so when, in 1893, the factory inspector required an improvement in the ventilation of the offices and works of the Company, the Manager suggested that the adoption of electric light might meet the difficulty. (Not many years previously the Southampton Electric Light Company had opened a small generating station in Back of the Walls.)

The progress of the *Echo* was such that in the year 1898 it gave birth to a sports weekly, the *Football Echo*, about which we shall have more to say in a later chapter, and two years after that, in 1900, it produced another lusty infant in the *Bournemouth Echo*. The latter began in a very modest way with a single-deck printing press housed in a former drill hall in Holdenhurst Road.[1] In those days the famous Hampshire seaside resort had a population of some 47,000. Today the *Evening Echo, Bournemouth*, serves an urban community of over a quarter of a million souls, besides scores of towns and villages scattered throughout west Hampshire and east Dorset, and is published from a fine modern building on Richmond Hill which is one of the landmarks of the locality.

Provincial newspaper offices at the beginning of the century, however, were seldom fine or modern. The *Southern Echo*'s at 52 Above Bar was fairly typical, no doubt. A young reporter from the North who joined the staff at about this time and was later to become successively Editor, General Manager and Chairman of the Company, William Arthur Gleave, recalled premises which were old, dilapidated and rat-ridden. "Indeed", he wrote, "a fine old tom-cat proved himself one of the most

----

[1] See also Chapter 11.

useful members of the staff! The machinery, mostly second-hand, was slow and cumbersome, and the working conditions extremely difficult."

In 1904 the board, whose Chairman was now Mr. W. Frank Perkins, decided to rebuild the premises in Above Bar, and in the following year the shareholders were told that "satisfactory progress has been made . . . and the general improvement in the Buildings is most marked". Commenting on this event twenty years later, in its Centenary number, the *Hampshire Advertiser* said: "When it was decided to build larger premises the Company made up its mind to do the thing so well that the new headquarters should rank among the finest buildings of the kind outside London and the larger provincial cities. . . . The whole idea was a bold and splendid one, and it had the result of not only giving the Company premises that newspaper experts still often visit to admire, but of greatly improving the appearance of Above Bar. Moreover, the buildings were planned with an eye to the future, in the confidence that the Company would go from success to success. Time has shown that that confidence was fully justified. . . ."

The new premises – in Above Bar – served the Company well until they were destroyed by fire during an air-raid on Southampton on the night of Saturday, November 30, 1940.

No record has survived of the cost of the new headquarters, but there is a board minute dated July 31, 1906, which states that the offices at 43-45 Above Bar would be insured for £12,500 (increased to £17,250 later in the year). At the same time, Henry King – now Managing Director – reported that the *Advertiser* office, 29 High Street, was still insured for £6,000 and suggested that "in view of the altered conditions arising from the removal of all the machinery", he should ask the insurance company for a reduced rate.

The present writer first entered the Above Bar building as a junior reporter straight from school in the late 20s, and still recalls his first impressions of a front office with a mahogany counter, like an old-established family bank; tiled passages and creaking lift – last touches of modernity, no doubt, in 1906, when the office was opened; crowded reporters' room on the first floor, looking down on the traffic of Above Bar; and behind it the sub-editors' department, where the silence was broken every minute or two by the despatch of copy down the pneumatic tube; a tiny "Creed" room where an ex-Signaller, "Tug" Wilson, transformed miles of punched tape into copy; and at the top of the building a board room of Edwardian ambience, where an oil painting representing a scene of martyrdom from the Reformation period looked down in anguish on the heads of the directors. (It should perhaps be explained that this *sanctum sanctorum* was entered by mere juniors only on Saturday afternoons, when the *Football Echo* was being produced and every telephone in the building – even the one in the board room – had to be manned by a copy-taker.)

Having established an up-to-date base for the Company's activities in Southampton, the board next turned its attention to the needs of the evening paper in Bournemouth. In October, 1906, the Chairman personally inspected the offices of the *Bournemouth Observer*, and it was decided to await the removal or liquidation of that weekly before attempting to purchase the premises. The Manager was later authorised to make an offer, "not exceeding £10,000". In the following February the deal was concluded and the premises in central Bournemouth known as Observer Chambers were obtained for £9,500. Mr. King's first task was to find out whether "such news-paper and jobbing machinery as we require could be placed on the present machine floor so as to reserve the Bijou Hall for letting off, and further to report whether by altering the ground-floor offices sufficient accommodation for the staff can be obtained, so that the whole of the first-floor offices could be let off".

In the April the Chairman asked Henry King to lunch at his New Forest home, Boldre Bridge House, and in this pleasantly relaxed atmosphere they opened the tenders for alterations to the Bournemouth premises. It was decided to accept Mr. F. Osman's – for £2,582.

One of the chief subjects discussed by the Chairman and the Managing Director as they strolled in the grounds of the Perkins home that late April day in 1907 was the form of power to be used at Bournemouth. Should they go on to the electric mains or continue to make their own current? They decided on the latter course, and the board agreed that for this purpose a new dynamo and gas engine should be bought.

The Company moved into the new premises – 2 Albert Road, Bournemouth – on May 18, 1908. In the following year the annual report stated that "the alterations and re-equipment of the Bournemouth Premises have now been completed, and the Directors congratulate the Shareholders on the result". The board also took the opportunity of recommending that "the amount standing to the credit of Premium on Ordinary Shares, amounting to £1,792, be disposed of by transferring £1,000 to the Reserve Fund, bringing that Account up to £8,500, and by writing the balance of £792 off the value of the *Bournemouth Daily Echo* Premises". The dividend that year stood at 14 per cent.

By now the Company's original headquarters, 29 High Street, Southampton, had been let and the registered office transferred to Above Bar. The old-established furniture firm of Shepherd and Hedger was for many years the company's tenant.

An item which turns up in the minutes during this period suggests that the Company was extending its transport system: "Mr. King reported that he had purchased a horse at Aldridge's Repository for 24 gns." In the Jubilee supplement of the *Southern Echo* (August 30, 1938) Captain A. E. Jones, M.C., the Editor, who had joined the staff as a reporter in 1898, recalled the early and somewhat primitive means used to distribute the paper:

"The *Echo* was printed on a flat-bed machine, which meant that only two pages could be printed at a time, and then they were transferred to another machine to be cut and folded. This laborious process occupied about an hour, and at eight o'clock 6,000 copies were ready for distribution to the horde of boys who thronged the tiny publishing room. There was no difficulty in supplying the centre of the town, but to get the papers to the suburbs of Shirley, Swaythling and Bitterne apparently presented a problem, which was solved by the employment of hand-trucks. In this way was the first edition of the *Southern Daily Echo* distributed to the public. . . . Ambition born of initial success, and experience, inspired the proprietor to extend his field of influence and to improve upon the original means of transport. So horse-trams and 'growlers' were used to supply the town, and the railway was requisitioned to get the paper to rural districts, which soon commenced to clamour for supplies. . . ."

The record of a horse having been purchased is evidence that by 1907, at least, the Company had one delivery van in service; probably it had several. But a good many years were to pass before the horse was displaced by the internal combustion engine. As late as 1911 the management reported to the board that, "having been in communication with 22 of the leading newspapers in this country with reference to the comparative cost and utility of motor traction compared with horse-drawn vehicles, it was found that on the whole there was a strong consensus of opinion against the former".

These were significant years in the development of the port – years which saw the transfer of the White Star Line's express transatlantic service from Liverpool to Southampton. The first of the White Star liners to make the southern port its terminal was the *Adriatic* (1907); she was followed by, the *Oceanic*, the *Olympic* (1911) and the ill-fated *Titanic* (1912). As the *Echo* explained when it reported the opening of the Trafalgar Graving Dock in 1905, Southampton was now practically the only place on the English seaboard where "the leviathans which are the feature of modern steamer construction can be received". The Docks' new owners, the London and South Western Railway

Company, had every reason to congratulate themselves. At a luncheon held on October 23, 1905, the Chairman, Sir Charles Scotter, summed up the situation in these words:

"The Prince of Wales Dock, opened in 1895, was 750 feet long, and was then considered the largest graving dock in the world. The Company thought, and everybody thought, that it would be sufficient to take not only the largest steamers afloat, but that they would be safe for the next twenty years. That was only ten years ago, and today they had opened a dock 875 feet long, upon which they had spent £300,000. Some people might say, 'Why build such a big dock when there are no ships afloat that can fill it?' Well, they had been in the habit in the L. & S. W. R. Company of looking ahead. They were told that the American transport trade would be carried on with 10,000-ton ships, yet now there were 20,000-ton ships, and he believed he was right in saying that within the last few weeks a German vessel of no less than 27,500 tons had been in the port. They anticipated even larger vessels. . . ."

The coming of the *Adriatic* two years later was an occasion of public rejoicing, and occupied many columns of the *Echo*. The liner's presence in the port, the newspaper remarked, signified much more than "the vanguard of four mammoth steamships carrying a certain number of passengers and boasting gigantic dimensions." It marked a triumph of considerable magnitude for Southampton in the great struggle between that port and Liverpool for recognition as the terminus for transatlantic traffic. Southampton's geographical position and facilities gave it an advantage that none could fail to recognise:

"What did the White Star people themselves admit in their official announcement of the change? They stated that 'the reason for taking this important step is due simply and solely to meet the growing demand of travellers that facilities should be provided to enable them to embark and disembark at either a Continental or British port, thus obviating the necessity of crossing the Channel'. Although this announcement was couched in terms that were intended to hurt the feelings of

Liverpool as little as possible, its meaning is clear beyond the possibility of misconstruction; it implies that Liverpool is not a convenient port for transatlantic travellers today; that Southampton is."

It was not only glory that the *Adriatic* was bringing to Southampton, but also money and employment. The decision of the White Star Line to use the port was responsible for the famous shipbuilding and repairing firm of Harland and Wolff opening a branch in the docks. No wonder the bells of Holy Rood rang a welcome! No wonder the main streets were illuminated, and the Mayor and Corporation set out in a paddle-steamer to greet the great liner as she steamed up Southampton Water!

In its issue of May 31, 1907, the *Echo* was able to report: "Southampton's welcome to the *Adriatic* last evening did justice to the town and to the shipping company who are making the port their home. When her bow hove in sight a mighty cheer rent the air from the crowds on Hythe Pier and in the Docks. Soon after 7 o'clock a clear view of the vessel's bow was obtained, and close beside her was the *Princess Helena*, with the Mayor and Corporation on board. There was no mistaking the cheers sent up all around and responded to by the steam valve of the *Adriatic*."

Once again the bigwigs were wisely wagging their heads and prophesying a great future for the port of Southampton. Among them was the borough's M.P., Colonel Ivor Philipps, who, at a luncheon on board the *Adriatic*, admonished all concerned not to make the mistake the German Emperor made when he ordered the construction of Kiel Canal, through which the *Dreadnought* could not now pass. "They must make their harbour fit to take the ships of the future; there was no reason why they should draw the line at the *Adriatic*."

No reason at all. Four years later the *Hampshire Advertiser*, in its issue of June 17, 1911, reported that the previous Wednesday had been a red-letter day in the history of the port, for then the *Olympic*, the mammoth 45,000-ton White Star liner, had sailed on her maiden voyage to New York. "It was a proud day for Southampton", declared the weekly in an editorial, "to witness the splendid facilities that enabled the biggest ship in the world to depart triumphantly and with that dignity so characteristic of all big ships; . . . the whole achievement stands unparalleled in the shipping world. Southampton is eventually to become the home of three vessels of the *Olympic* class. Her twin sister, the *Titanic*, will be ready by about the end of the year. The third leviathan has yet to be built, and the triplets will represent a capital of about £4,500,000. This is an enormous sum for a single weekly service, but it is the inevitable result of the demand for big ships and luxury travel. . . . It is with a feeling of honest pride that Southampton can claim the biggest ships and the largest and deepest docks in the world."

The coming of the *Titanic* aroused nothing like the enthusiasm with which the people of Southampton had welcomed the *Adriatic* five years previously. As the *Hampshire Independent* remarked, the world's latest and biggest ship steamed up the silent waters of the Solent and docked at Southampton "quietly and unostentatiously, without any blare of trumpets". Nevertheless, the presence of this great vessel in the port was a source of considerable satisfaction to the townspeople. The *Titantic*, after all, was something special. To quote the *Independent* again, so intense had the competition in transatlantic passenger traffic become that "each new ocean queen must surpass her rival in some respect. Luxury and speed are today the two great factors which attract the aristocracy and plutocracy. . . . And so we find the *Titanic* able to offer something which none of her rivals can; indeed, she makes her appeal to the pleasure-seeking millionaire who finds comfort in the thought that he is saving time. . . ."

Those who sailed in the *Titanic* on her maiden (and only) voyage from Southampton may have been in a hurry, but many never even reached their destination. At 2.20 a.m. on April 15, 1912, she went to the bottom of the Atlantic after striking an iceberg at full-speed. Of the 2,224 souls on board, 1,513 perished. The cruel sea robbed hundreds of Southampton homes of their bread-winners. Undoubtedly the loss of the *Titanic* was the worst tragedy in the history of the port, and the biggest news story which, up till then, had been covered by the newspapers belonging to the Hampshire Advertiser Company. The files of the *Southern Echo* and the *Advertiser* for that period were destroyed in the war, but the *Independent* files escaped the flames, and it is from these we take the following comment:

"The civilised world is suffering from the shock of a huge calamity, the sorrow attending which is brought home with particular force to our own town of Southampton. The loss of the White Star liner *Titanic* is a disaster of a magnitude which is unparalleled in the annals of the Mercantile Marine. Great disasters there have been, spreading bereavement and sorrow over a wide circle, but nothing so huge as this has ever happened before. The *Titanic*, the largest ship in the world, only on Wednesday last week left Southampton on her first voyage with all the pomp and circumstance attendant on her reputation as the Queen of the Ocean; early on Monday morning she sank off the Banks of Newfoundland and became the coffin of her officers, crew and male passengers. . . ."

It was remarked at the time that when the great vessel moved down the river under the bright spring sunshine, no hint or premonition of impending misfortune marred her memorable send-off. Yet there was one such incident. . . .

"There were a few anxious moments", reported the *Independent*, "before the *Titanic* got under weigh. As the ship passed the end of the Test Quay, where the *Oceanic* and the American liner *New York* were moored, the disturbance caused by such an immense displacement of water put such a strain on the stern ropes of the American vessel that she began to swing into the fairway. For a moment a collision seemed imminent, but the *Titanic*'s screws were instantly stopped, and a tug thereupon towed the *New York* out of the danger zone."

CHAPTER 8

Pictorial Journalism

THE COMPANY'S REPORT for 1908 stated that it would be necessary to consider at the annual general meeting the appointment of a Managing Director, as Mr. King's term would expire on that day. Henry had been the chief executive of the Company since 1877, when he succeeded his father, and had seen it grow from a small weekly newspaper concern into one of the most influential publishing firms in the South of England, with two evenings and three weeklies (including the *Football Echo*) to its credit, and one of the finest newspaper offices in the provinces. His greatest achievement, surely, had been his successful negotiations with Passmore Edwards for the purchase of the *Southern Echo*.

The board had no hesitation in recommending the shareholders to reappoint him as Managing Director for a further term of six years at a salary of £1,150 per annum, "provided that his health permits him to continue to discharge the duties of his office". Evidently he had shown signs of failing powers; two years later he was dead. At their meeting on November 19, 1910, the directors decided not to elect another Managing Director in the place of Mr. King, but to take upon themselves (so the board minute reads) some of the responsibilities of that office and to appoint a General Manager. Meanwhile, they would consider the election of a new director and call a meeting to inform the shareholders of the proposed changes and to make fresh arrangements for the remuneration of directors.

There was never any real doubt about Henry King's

successor. He was James H. Goldsmith, who had been Deputy Manager since the Company acquired the *Southern Echo* and the *Independent* in 1891. Appointed General Manager and Editor-in-chief with effect from June 24, 1910, his contract provided that "in the event of his leaving the Company's service he was not to practise in the counties of Hampshire and Dorset".

At the same time William Arthur Gleave was appointed Editor of the *Southern Echo* and assistant to Mr. Goldsmith; Mr. Lashmore and Mr. Ley were confirmed in their editorships of the *Independent* and *Advertiser* respectively; Mr. H. J. Cheverton was appointed Manager of the *Bournemouth Echo*; and Mr. Ross King was confirmed as London Manager.

Mr. Gleave, a Lancastrian, had started his career on the *Warrington Guardian* and, before moving to Southampton at the age of twenty-two, had become chief reporter on the *Stockport Chronicle*. He joined the *Echo* as Sports Editor in 1894 and launched the *Football Echo*, of which he was first Editor, in 1898. Mr. Cheverton, an East Anglian, gained his early experience on the *Essex Weekly News*, and was appointed to the commercial staff of the *Bournemouth Echo* when it was founded in 1900.

It was in the year 1910 that the Chairman of the Company, Mr. W. Frank Perkins, was elected Conservative M.P. for the New Forest Division. Naturally, the board congratulated him, and in returning thanks the new Member "expressed his appreciation of the valuable help he had received from the Press". Here perhaps it is appropriate to quote from a memoir which his daughter, Mrs. Mary Hopkirk, wrote by way of introduction to the *Catalogue of the Walter Frank Perkins Agricultural Library*, published in 1961 by the University of Southampton:

"His parents, Walter and Mary Louisa Perkins, belonged to an old New Forest family whose roots lay in the Avon Valley. The baby's grandfather, Richard Perkins, had settled in South-ampton on his marriage in 1820 and founded a large family, most of whom played a prominent part in the civic, professional and business life of the rapidly developing town. Sir Frederick Perkins, the baby's uncle, was Mayor when Lord Palmerston arrived from Broadlands to open the new and comparatively humble – but much-needed – adult education centre (the Hartley Institution, embryo of the University of Southampton). . . .

"The children spent long summers at Wimpson Farm in Millbrook (then entirely rural), and later at Stoke Farm, Bishopstoke, which their father rented, and it was there that the little boy acquired his love of farming in the days before mechanisation – watching the corn cut with sickles and the hay falling under the scythes. . . .

"As a small child he attended a day school kept by a Miss Alford in Hill Lane, and later went to the Forest School at Snaresbrook. Meanwhile, his father bought a seemingly derelict house, then known as Abbott's Park, on the edge of the town, rehabilitated it and restored its former name of Portswood House. The family lived there until 1912.

"In 1885, Walter Frank entered the Royal Agricultural College at Cirencester, whence he emerged after two years with the Senior certificate of the Royal Agricultural Society of England, the first-class certificate of the Highland and Agricultural Society of Scotland (taking the first place of all candidates in agriculture), the first-class certificate and silver medal of the Royal Agricultural Society of Ireland, and the College's own diploma with honours. He passed second out of fifty-six in the land agency sub-division of the Surveyors' Institution, and soon afterwards became a Professional Associate.

"At an early age he became a bibliophile, specialising in books on agriculture, botany and forestry, which were then of interest only to a very limited section of book-collectors, and could be obtained comparatively easily and inexpensively.

"On leaving Cirencester he joined his father's business as a surveyor, and while in practice became a Fellow of the Surveyors' Institution. . . .

"Prior to his marriage, he made long tours of Canada and the United States, and went round the world. In 1901 he settled at Boldre Bridge House, near Lymington. In 1910 he entered Parliament as Member for the New Forest, having won the seat by a record majority, and he was unopposed in the two ensuing general elections. He retired from politics in 1922, and thenceforward devoted himself to literary and agricultural pursuits. . . ."

Mr. Frank Perkins's association with the Hampshire Advertiser Company began in 1897, when he joined the board as junior director. But, as he himself wrote in an autobiographical article he contributed to the firm's house magazine, long before that he was closely interested in the Company and its affairs, "because my father, as a director, and afterwards as Chairman, was constantly calling on Mr. Henry King, our Manager. As a child, I remember being taken on a Friday night, after a performance at the old theatre in French Street, to the *Advertiser* office in the High Street, to see the paper being printed."

★   ★   ★

Early in Mr. Goldsmith's term of office negotiations were opened with the G.P.O. and National Telephone Company for the installation of a private line between the Southampton and Bournemouth offices, the rent being £250 per annum. At the same time arrangements were made for an additional deck and a stop press device to be added to the Hoe single roll printing press at Southampton at a cost of some £1,300, and an order was placed for a Linotype jobbing machine at a cost of £747. Small beer, perhaps, judged by modern standards, but evidence of considerable enterprise in the world of pre-1914 provincial journalism.

There was at this time a general review of wages and salaries, and among those who received increases was Mr. E. G. Burnett, who had succeeded Edney C. Curtis as Secretary of the Company in 1906. The secretarial duties had grown considerably over the years, but the post was not to become a full-time

Above: The second office of the *Bournemouth Daily Echo*, Observer Chambers, 2 Albert Road (1908).

Right: The *Bournemouth Echo*'s third office, Old Christchurch Road (1921).

The *Dorset Evening Echo*'s post-war premises in St. Thomas Street.

First *Dorset Daily Echo* office, St. Mary Street, Weymouth.

one until World War II. (Mr. Burnett, who first acted as accountant to the Hampshire Advertiser Company in 1896, was a partner in the Southampton firm of J. J. Burnett & Sons, chartered accountants.)

An important development occurred in 1911. A photo-engraving plant was opened at the Southampton office, and for the first time half-tone blocks began to appear in the Company's publications. In April, 1912, a new illustrated weekly was launched, the *Southampton Pictorial*. It was an immediate success. The publishers promised snapshots of sporting events, liners entering the port, flower shows and garden parties, street incidents and curiosities of all kinds. There were to be specially written literary features, too, the first being a history of Southampton's part in the great South African War. Sales of the *Pictorial* during its first three weeks totalled 20,000, which was considered an excellent figure, and by June the circulation had settled down to a respectable 4,000 a week. In September Mr. Goldsmith was able to inform the board that the new weekly had now been permanently enlarged to twenty pages, and that its revenue during the past six months had been "extremely gratifying". Unfortunately, however, this new-style pictorial journalism was not without its dangers for the men who went after the news pictures. In January, 1913, the General Manager regretfully reported that the photographer, Mr. Carter (known far and wide as "Sticky"), had been very badly burned about the face and hands while manipulating a flashlight apparatus at the Grand Theatre.

The performance of the firm's other weekly papers came under review during this period. The sales of the *Independent*, it was stated, had gone up since the firm had decided to cease publishing the *Woolston Independent* – a short-lived experiment. The *Advertiser*'s circulation had also increased as a result of reducing the price to 1d. the previous year. But it was felt that the latter was capable of a good deal of improvement from a literary and popular point of view. Mr. Goldsmith's solution was "to engage a descriptive writer at an estimated annual

F

outlay of £150, for which expenditure there would probably be no immediate return". The board evidently agreed with him, for soon afterwards Douglas Newton joined the staff. This well-known novelist was succeeded by the late E. A. Mitchell, who made a lasting mark on the *Southern Echo* as a note-writer of charm and erudition, a dramatic critic of perception and fairness and a leader-writer of shrewd judgment and deep personal conviction. Probably no member of the editorial staff at Southampton has ever won so much affection from his colleagues as "Mike" Mitchell.

If the weeklies sometimes occasioned anxiety in those days, the same could certainly not be said of the firm's two evenings. In the spring of 1912 it was noted that "as outcome of the *Titanic* disaster the circulation of the *Southern Echo* and *Bournemouth Echo* for the week ending April 20 was phenomenally large, the total output of the two offices being 420,000 copies, which constituted a new record". The influence and popularity of the two papers was also shown by the fact that appeals in their columns for the Ray of Sunshine Fund (to relieve destitution) were raising some £350 a year.

In the summer of 1912 the possibility of changing over from horse-drawn transport to "some form of motor traction" was again considered. "The Manager submitted various specifications for motors, but the directors decided to leave the question of motor-traction until more suitable cars were on the market." As an interim measure, they decided to buy another cob.

The following year brought change and expansion. The installation of extra Linotype machines made it possible for the firm to abolish night work in the Southampton composing room, and the engagement of a relief reporter during the summer months enabled the "literary department" of the *Southern Echo* to enjoy extended holidays. The growth of the Company's business was such that the Above Bar premises were already, after seven years, proving inadequate. The only alternative appeared to be to add another storey to the printing department or to acquire the cottages in Spa Road and use their site for an extension to the premises. In April, 1913, Messrs. Waller and King, estate agents, were instructed to negotiate for the purchase of the cottages. Soon afterwards the Company's original home, 29 High Street, was sold to Scrase's Brewery for £7,500. That year a dividend of 14 per cent. was declared and the shareholders received an additional bonus of 5 per cent. It was a period of steady progress through calm waters, but it was to prove a calm before the worst storm in living memory.

CHAPTER 9

The Kaiser's War

"IMPERIAL MADMAN OR BULLY – OR BOTH?" Under this heading the *Hampshire Independent*, in its issue of August 8, 1914, published its first leading article of the war. The views which it expressed were no doubt shared by the *Advertiser* and the *Southern Echo*, but their files for this crucial period are missing. Europe, remarked the *Independent*, was now faced with a conflict which had not had its equal since the days of Napoleon. And for what? To satisfy the mad ambition of a monarch who, ever since the day he ascended the throne of Germany, had kept the world in a state of perpetual unrest.

"What a reflection it is upon our boasted civilisation", the leader continued, "that in these modern days when Peace Celebrations, Peace Temples and the settlement of international disputes by arbitration are constantly talked of and advocated, it should be within the power of one man to sound the tocsin of war and set the whole Continent ablaze with its horrors, and to paralyse the whole of the world's commerce and financial stability. The Kaiser has proved himself to be a truculent, aggressive bully; but he has not learnt the lesson that while 'it is excellent to have a giant's strength, it is tyrannous to use it like a giant'. The nightmare that, in spite of all the Emperor's hypocritical professions of peace, has haunted the nations year by year is dispelled, and Germany is at this moment at war with Russia, France, Great Britain, and the little Kingdom of Belgium, with Austria-Hungary as a backer up if needs be under the conditions of the Triple Alliance. . . ."

The *Independent* correctly expressed the general mood when it declared that there was not "a man among us who will counsel cowardice or shirk from the responsibilities which the Government has undertaken. The Nation is united; the Empire is united; Great Britain beyond the seas is eager to help the Mother Country. The salvation of Western Europe is in the balance, and Great Britain and France will (by the aid of a Higher Power from which the Kaiser claims special patronage) do their utmost to defeat an unprincipled aggressor. May God defend the right!"

If the war had aroused patriotic fervour, it had also created a certain amount of panic. Almost immediately there was a run on the food-shops, and prices began to soar. From the House of Commons on August 6 the M.P. for the New Forest Division wrote a letter on "Our Plain Duty" for publication in the various journals belonging to the Company of which he was Chairman.

"For the information of your readers, I venture to state that there are now ample supplies of wheat, meat and other provisions; ships laden with supplies are close to our shores; and now that national provision has been made for the insurance of ships and cargoes, there is every reason to be assured that supplies will be maintained in sufficiency, and probably in abundance, as long as the war lasts. Our wheat harvest" – and here Mr. Perkins wrote with the authority of a scientific farmer – "is officially returned as 'above average'; and today's report of our potato crop is that it is sufficient for a whole year's consumption. Some spasmodic rises in the prices of certain articles of food are inevitable, but they are provoked by the mischievous and selfish policy of accumulating private stores. I know that the Government is prepared to put an end to this artificial inflation of prices, should it continue, by acquiring the whole stock of food and fixing the prices at which it can be retailed; but I hope the common sense of the nation will make this drastic step unnecessary. Retailers can be of great help in the matter by refusing to sell large quantities of provisions to any individual. . . ."

The war had the immediate effect of making Southampton, as the No. 1 Military Embarkation Port, one of the busiest places in the kingdom, and at the same time of spreading distress and unemployment among a considerable section of the inhabitants. The Docks were at once placed under military control, and for a while all commercial shipping was paralysed. Soon it became necessary to open a special fund for the relief of hardship caused by the war – hailed by the *Independent* as "a wise decision on the part of the Mayor to take steps in time to cope with the situation".

By the end of that never-to-be-forgotten August the *Independent* was busy assessing Hampshire's, and especially Southampton's, contribution to the war effort. "Our county", it said, "has contributed its fair quota of well-disciplined men who have responded to the call to arms either by volunteering for active service abroad or to assist in home defence, and the smallest of our villages are proudly recording, on their little rolls of fame, the names of their sons who have thus responded to the call from King and Country.

"Southampton especially is very much in the public eye just now, but though much of what has been done during the last fortnight or three weeks was visible to local eyes, there was a veil of secrecy over the preparations for the despatch of the Expeditionary Force which, now that the thousands of men comprising it have been safely landed on French soil, has been lifted. . . . The railway and docks have been handed over to the military authorities. And though the passage of thousands of soldiers and horses through our streets, with siege and hospital trains, and the rushing by of hundreds of huge motor-vans laden with stores and supplies of all kinds, afforded evidence that stirring events were at hand, no one except those concerned in the matter really knew what was going on."

According to the *Independent*, the townspeople were particularly proud of the fact that a Southampton man, Admiral Sir John Rushworth Jellicoe (later Earl Jellicoe), had assumed supreme command of the Home Fleet. It was recalled that this great sailor was a member of a well-known Southampton family, some of whom were still resident in the neighbourhood. "He was born in the town", continued the *Independent*, "and is the son of Captain J. H. Jellicoe, who at the close of his sea-going career was Commodore-Captain of the Royal Mail Steam Packet Company, and is now a director of that great shipping undertaking. Southampton may well be proud of her distinguished son, for whom it is fervently hoped greater honours are in store by victories won in the present naval campaign in defence of his country's honour, dignity and safety." (What the writer of this note forgot to add is that Jellicoe was educated at a local school, Banister Court, which was originally intended for the sons of Merchant Navy officers.)

What effect the war would have on the fortunes of the Company was at first uncertain. The *Independent* (and presumably this applied to the *Echos* and the *Advertiser* as well) was immediately reduced in size, "as a necessary precaution against possible scarcity of newspaper owing to the conflict". With a prospect before them of small papers and therefore of reduced revenue, the directors might have been forgiven if they had adopted a somewhat negative attitude in those early days of the war, but to their credit they did nothing of the kind. The war was not yet two months old when the annual general meeting of the Company was held on September 28, and the board took the opportunity of recommending the inauguration of a Benevolent and Pension Fund for the employees "by setting aside the sum of £1,000, which, it is hoped, will be added to from time to time out of the profits of the Company".

Another interesting item on the agenda was a plan to buy 13 Portland Terrace, Southampton, and the adjoining plot of land, to provide a site for a garage, workshops and store. Evidently the Company had at last gone over to "motor-traction" for its transport! At this meeting the death was announced of Robert Scott Hankinson, who had been a director for a quarter of a century. Mr. John Cornelius Moberly was elected in his place, and at the same time Colonel Sir Edwin Perkins (later to be Conservative M.P. for Southampton) joined the board as fourth director.

In spite of many difficulties, the dividend on the Company's share capital never dropped below 10 per cent. during the four years of war. Typical was the statement in the annual report for 1916 that the firm's business was "being efficiently carried out, notwithstanding the fact that 39 of their employees are now serving in H.M. Forces".

Unfortunately detailed records of the war years are missing, but the atmosphere of the editorial departments at Southampton during this period is vividly and wittily conveyed by these notes kindly contributed by one who was a junior reporter on the *Southern Echo* at this time:[1]

"With the outbreak of war in 1914 it might almost be said that the *Echo* came to a temporary standstill, for nearly all sources of news automatically dried up. Meetings and customary celebrations were hurriedly abandoned and even the theatre closed for a period, as touring companies were unable to fulfil dates, owing to the congestion on the railways, which had been commandeered by the military for the transport of troops and guns and ammunition.

"The editorial staff were flung into a miserable state of dejection, sitting around the reporters' room waiting for something to turn up. Starving for news, as Freddie Prince-White put it. Prince-White was a singularly live-wire journalist with a real flair for a good story, and, after serving with the 5th Hants in India, came back to join the staff of the *Daily Mail*.

"A. E. Jones, chief reporter and Sports Editor, found things unendurable, for the war caused the suspension of all forms of sport for the duration. He quickly wearied of the collapse of the sporting world, and decided to enlist in the Royal Welch Fusiliers and apply for a commission. Later he was gazetted Captain and won the M.C. for a conspicuous act of gallantry

[1] Mr. Stanley Heather, who left journalism to enter the acting profession and is now a civil servant.

and was twice mentioned in dispatches. His return to the *Echo* at the conclusion of the war savoured something of see 'the conquering hero comes!'

"Overriding the entire activities of the office, of course, was Mr. James Henry Goldsmith, General Manager and Editor-in-chief. Clad always in a brown striped suit with white waistcoat displaying a gold albert chain, and patent leather boots embraced by grey spats, he typified the miniature tycoon. A waxed moustache attaining almost pencil-like precision, coupled with a Midland accent, added somewhat to his assumed air of ferocity. If rather uncomfortably 'mauled' at the monthly board meeting he would bounce into the reporters' room and hurl a broadside at the entire staff for 'incompetence, inefficiency and downright carelessness'; then flounce out of the room, giving the door a mighty slam to emphasise his departure.

"'Well, I hope you chaps feel better after that,' Freddie Stevens[1] (then in charge of the reporters' room) would say. Stevens was a hard-working, solidly reliable journalist, and a first-class shorthand writer. He was always sufficiently generous to pass on a word of praise to colleagues if he thought their work merited it. His book on the New Forest attained widespread popularity and was much sought after for its absolute authenticity.

"Without fear of contradiction, it is safe to say that the most colourful personality on the staff at that time was Thomas James Monk, a massive chunk of a man who hailed from Bath, which he declared to be 'the finest city in the world'. Bearing a striking resemblance to the late G. K. Chesterton, he became quite a notable character about the town, so much so that passers-by would often point and exclaim, 'Look! He's on the *Echo*.' His gift for the swear-word was wellnigh incredible!

"Sub-editor 'Mike' Mitchell (as he was always called) was

[1] F. E. Stevens, who died in 1951, was the last Editor of the *Hampshire Advertiser*, which ceased publication in 1940, when the Company's Southampton offices were destroyed.

one of those quiet, charming and intellectual persons who made a newspaper office a joy to work in. Never endowed with robust health, he steadfastly maintained a courageous and philosophical outlook on life, and under the pen-name of Townsman contributed some very delightful and interesting articles on local topics. A keen lover of the theatre, he had long nursed a secret ambition – to be a successful playwright. Several times he toyed with the idea and wrote one or two plays, but the success he dreamt about never came his way. 'Mike' appeared indifferent, but most of the staff knew that behind the pretence of not caring there lurked a deep and heartfelt disappointment.

"If ever there was a man who liked to 'pop' into the reporters' room for a quiet pipe of 'baccy and a joke it was William Arthur Gleave, Editor and Assistant Manager to the great James Henry – 'Billy', as he was always known to the staff. Ample of proportion and a connoisseur of good food and liquor, he gave the impression of being a comedian off-stage whose features still carried traces of his humorous calling. Unfailingly jovial and always ready for a laugh, he could, nevertheless, be the last word in managerial sternness when the occasion required it. One afternoon he related with great gusto how on the previous night he had heard two women in a tramcar indulge in more scandal in ten minutes than he had listened to in the whole course of his previous life! His verdict on Frank Benson, the celebrated Shakespearian actor-manager, whom he had recently seen at the Grand as Brutus in *Julius Caesar*, was: 'The rottenest actor I've ever witnessed.' Billy's critical opinions were diverting, but not always flattering. . . .

"Early dusk one evening nearly the entire *Echo* staff were clustered at the office windows. Some stood on tables, some on chairs, others even outside on the window-ledges. Down below in Above Bar crowds thronged the pavements. The first contingents of the Old Contemptibles were marching past on their way to embark for France at the docks. Having encamped on the Common overnight, they now came by, singing

'Tipperary' and shouting 'Are we downhearted?' And back would come the thunderous response, 'No!' The flower of manhood they were called – England's answer to the Kaiser's insolent challenge. Most were never to return. Lustily the *Echo* staff cheered them and shouted, 'Let 'em have it, boys.'

"Later on another crowd was to congregate near the office to scan the huge poster displayed in the window announcing that H.M.S. *Hampshire* had been sunk, and that Kitchener and his staff were drowned. Venerated as Kitchener then was, the news came like a hammer-blow of doom.

"As the war months dragged along, acute difficulties beset the *Echo*. The shortage of paper had reduced it to four small pages and copy had to be slashed to the minimum. 'Keep it down' was the daily exhortation. The depletion of staff, editorially, created insoluble problems in covering the many engagements which, with the impact of war receding, were now flooding in. Most of the younger members of the staff had left to enlist, and their places were taken by journalistic pupils. These young fellows were signed up for four-year apprentice-ships, commencing with a salary of 5s. a week for the first year, with a corresponding increase each succeeding one, so that at the end of the allotted agreement they were receiving the princely sum of £1 per week. Even their presence failed to do much to ease the heavy burden on the few remaining full-blown repor-ters who were left. This situation often brought forth explosive protests from Tommy Monk, who, on inspecting the diary, would angrily expostulate, 'Why not shove me down for every bloody engagement in the book?'

"In the second year of the war a bombshell, metaphorically speaking, exploded in the office. The *Southampton Pictorial*, a companion paper to the *Echo*, was prosecuted under the Def-fence of the Realm Act (D.O.R.A.) for publishing photographs calculated to furnish the enemy with useful information. Banner headlines appeared in the Echo: 'SOUTHAMPTON PICTORIAL PROSECUTED – FOR TAKING PICTURES AT RED CROSS FÊTE'. The alleged 'information to the enemy' actually consisted of harmless photos of a semi-military fête at the County Cricket Ground in aid of the Red Cross, at which wounded soldiers assisted. A long-drawn out hearing was held at the police court. The outcome was a fine, it being established that a technical offence only had been committed and that none of the information revealed would help the Germans to win the war.

"Many notabilities came to the town during the war whom the *Echo* had the privilege of reporting and interviewing. Included among them were David Lloyd George, the Prime Minister, Horatio Bottomley, Admiral King-Hall and Maude Royden, the suffragette. And at the Grand Theatre the paper was called upon to assess the histrionic talents of such well-known personalities as Fred Terry and Julia Neilson, Seymour Hicks, Lewis Waller, Matheson Lang, Lady Tree, Laurence Irving, Arthur Bourchier and Martin Harvey. It can truly be said that the *Echo* did its job magnificently during the years of World War I, and that the staff worked together with understanding, goodwill and complete accord. Not one edition was ever late or failed to appear."

CHAPTER 10

Jubilee

ON NOVEMBER 10, 1918, rumours were rife in Southampton – the kingdom's No. 1 Military Embarkation Port – that an armistice was imminent; they proved to be correct. The following day, at about a quarter to ten in the morning, the Mayor (Alderman – later Sir – Sidney Kimber) received the official news that hostilities were to cease from 11 a.m. that day. The dramatic sequence of events was later to be described by Sir Sidney in his autobiographical *Thirty-eight Years of Public Life in Southampton*:

"The tension had snapped. I found myself trembling with emotion when I opened my door to spread the news. The silence had gone. Outside the door was Chief Town Sergeant Braxton . . . fighting to keep back the crowd of Aldermen, Councillors and others in the narrow corridor, awaiting the joyful news. . . .

"It took what appeared to be hours for a way to be forced for me to get through the corridors and Council Chamber to the little balcony overlooking the street. . . . The street below was packed to capacity and every window was full of people and faces. The noise was terrific. . . .

"Our appearance secured a miraculous silence, and . . . I announced the Prime Minister's message. The effect was instantaneous. The crowd went stark, staring mad with emotion and delirium. Hats, gloves, newspapers, matchboxes were thrown into the air, cheering was spontaneous and men's and women's eyes were wet with streaming, happy tears, and there we all stood, waving our arms, looking at each other for several minutes before I attempted to get a hearing. . . .

"I thought the crowd would never disperse, although I think they would have gladly done so, to distribute the glad news to their relatives, but they were hemmed in by newcomers blocking their exits at Holy Rood and Town Quay. . . . By three o'clock everyone had left off work, the streets everywhere were filled with people marching along with flags and banners. . . . Hartley students carrying buckets, tin trays and bugles, British, French, Belgian, American and Italian soldiers and sailors, munition workers, Waacs, Wrens and others, paraded up and down the High Street, Above Bar and St. Mary's Street for a couple of hours. The whole scene was hilarious in its spontaneity. I heard afterwards that the ever changing pageant continued until midnight."

★   ★   ★

"The beastly business being now stopped", ran that evening's *Southern Echo* report of the Mayor's speech, "the thing uppermost in everyone's mind was relief and thankfulness. This cessation of hostilities was the finish, for there was no doubt that the downfall of Germany was assured, and there could be no country so silly, after the experience of death and misery through which the world had passed, as to start war again. . . ."

★   ★   ★

By the following spring most of the employees who had served in the Armed Forces had been demobilised. The time had come for a celebration, and it was Mr. Gleave who had the happy idea of holding a staff dinner at the South-Western Hotel to mark the Jubilee of the Hampshire Advertiser Company. This should have been held in the summer of 1914, but was postponed because of the war.

The day – April 21, 1919 – began with a cricket match between the Southampton and Bournemouth staffs – another of Mr. Gleave's inspirations. One of the directors, Dr. (later

Sir) Russell Bencraft,[1] captained the Bournemouth XI, and
Mr. Gleave led the home side. Southampton won by forty-five
runs.

That evening the staffs of the two offices dined amid the
Edwardian splendours of the South-Western, where glittering
chandeliers filled the spacious banqueting room with brilliant
light. In the absence of Mr. W. Frank Perkins – who had taken
advantage of an unexpected Parliamentary recess to go with
his family to Jersey for his first peace-time holiday – Dr.
Bencraft presided. For him it was a family occasion, for his
wife's father, as he explained, had been that Walter Perkins
who had been one of the founding directors of the Company
and had served on the board for forty years. The note struck by
Dr. Bencraft in his after-dinner speech showed that concern
for the employees which has always been a characteristic of the
Company.

They had two objects in view, he said. First, to look after the
interests of the shareholders and to ensure that they received a
fair return on the capital they had invested; and, second – and
far more important – to keep always in mind the welfare of the
people they employed. In Dr. Bencraft's opinion, "capital
was all very well, but in these days labour also has to be considered, and they would agree with him that the war had very
much altered all their views". He believed in shorter hours in
return for a fair day's effort.

What gave force to his words was his announcement that
the directors, with the unanimous consent of the shareholders,
had on the outbreak of the war opened a Benevolent and Pension
Fund. It was the object of the Company, Dr. Bencraft declared,
to ensure that the man who had put in long years of service
should never go down to the grave in want. They intended
that he should spend his last days in comfort and happiness.

Naturally, this was an occasion for compliments and
reminiscences. Dr. Bencraft took the opportunity to praise

[1] A fine cricketer in his day, and for many years President of the Hampshire County Cricket Club.

General Manager Goldsmith for his shrewdness ("no man could be more clever in making a bargain") and Mr. Gleave for his editorial ability, good temper and geniality. ("You have only to look at his cheery face to know what a good sort he is.")

Mr. E. G. Burnett, the Company Secretary, spoke of the debt they owed to the late Henry King, recalling that when negotiating for the purchase of the *Southern Echo* he had "practically waited on the doorstep and worried Mr. Passmore Edwards until he had acquired the undertaking". Mr. Goldsmith expressed gratitude to his board and praise for his staff. Mr. Cheverton, looking back to the days before the *Bournemouth Echo* was started, recalled that when the *Southern Echo* arrived each night at the seaside town "the clamour for copies was indescribable, so much so that people could not wait to pay for them, but actually stole bundles of papers. . . ." Mr. H. Lashmore, the veteran Editor of the *Hampshire Independent*, said that in 1860 when he first became associated with the paper it was printed on an old Napier machine, the motive power of which was provided by two men turning a wheel. . . . A solemn note was struck by Colonel E. K. Perkins (Director) when proposing "Those who served", to which Captain A. E. Jones, M.C. – just back from troubled Ireland, where he had been demobilised – responded on behalf of all ex-Servicemen present.

It was, as a leader in the *Independent* remarked, an historic occasion. For the Jubilee they had been celebrating did not indicate a life of only fifty years. The *Hampshire Advertiser* and the *Hampshire Independent* – once deadly political rivals, but now working in friendly and successful co-operation – had length of days far beyond that. "And", the editorial continued, "it may be said without ostentation that both journals are well fulfilling their purpose, and are living forces in the making of local history by the week-by-week recording of passing events in the extensive district covered by their large circulations. The *Southern Daily Echo*, an offshoot of the *Hampshire Independent*, and its sister, the *Bournemouth Daily Echo*, hardly need mention beyond the fact that they stand out

The headquarters of the *Evening Echo, Bournemouth*, on Richmond Hill. (Opened 1934: enlarged and modernised, 1961-2).

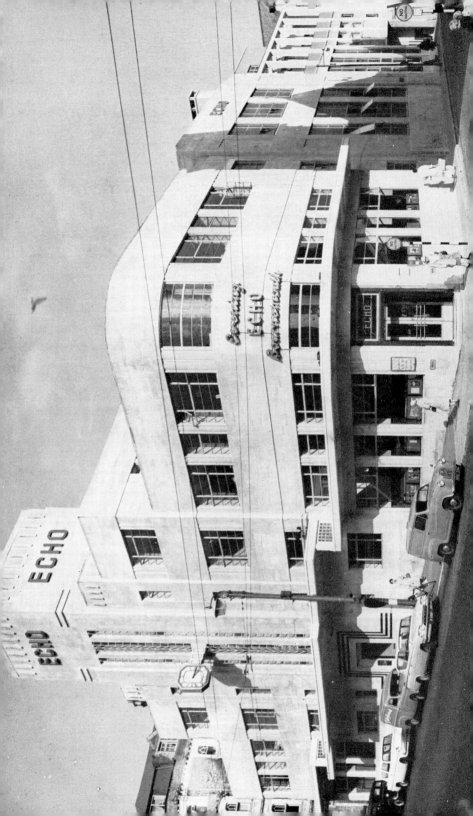

as the most successful journals and as monuments of local journalistic enterprise, and much the same may be said of the *Football Echo* – suspended during the war – and the *Southampton Pictorial*, the last-named a paper which has gained immense popularity."

The *Independent* "could not refrain from calling attention to the splendid record of long and faithful service of many of the Company's employees, to the sympathetic speeches made on the occasion of the commemoration dinner, and to the evident good feeling existing between employers and employees, a refreshing and gratifying fact in these days when so much is heard of unrest and dispute between capital and labour, arising so often out of a want of sympathy and non-recognition of the responsibility on the one side, and of appreciation on the other, of what capital means if labour is to have its due." (This reference to good labour-management relations was no empty rhetoric. Few companies have had such an excellent record in this respect as Southern Newspapers Limited, which throughout its long history has been involved in only two major stoppages – the General Strike of 1926, during which the firm's newspapers continued to be published, and the national printers' strike in 1959.)

In 1921 the *Dorset Daily Echo* was founded.[1] The Company's report for that year baldly states: "Offices have recently been opened at Dorchester and Weymouth in connection with the starting of the new daily paper, which has been styled the *Dorset Echo and Weymouth Dispatch*. This paper was first on sale to the public in the latter part of May this year."

It was against a background of post-war slump that the directors made this bold decision to expand the Company's circulation area in a westward direction. The headquarters of the new *Echo* were established in a former bank building in St. Mary Street, Weymouth, where the brass-railed counters gave the front office an imposing appearance. Here an enthusiastic

[1] Mr. A. R. Adlam, present Editor of the *Dorset Evening Echo*, has kindly supplied notes dealing with the history of that newspaper.

The company's branch in Winchester, now known as Echo House, was once a city hostelry, the Plough Inn. This historic building was adapted and re-opened as the *Southern Evening Echo*'s Winchester office in 1959.

G

staff of less than a dozen worked long hours to establish the paper against the opposition of the *Dorset Daily Press*, which had been founded by a Channel Islands newspaper company only four days after the first issue of the *Dorset Echo* had appeared. Weymouth, with a population of about 20,000 had more local papers at that time than any other town of its size – two evenings and three weeklies.

At Dorchester a former butcher's shop was converted into a branch office, manned by a reporter and advertisement clerk; and in the west of the county *Echo* interests were looked after by a free-lance journalist.

Printed on the Company's Bournemouth presses, the *Dorset Echo* of those days followed a familiar provincial evening newspaper format – a 27-inch column, with a width of seven or eight columns, according to the weight of news and advertising. Classified advertisements filled the front page. There was only one edition, late news being printed in the stop press space at the Weymouth office by a hand-operated fudge machine. At first motor-cycle combinations were used to transport the paper from Bournemouth to Weymouth; later it was sent by rail.

Nationally the news headlines of 1921 concerned the Irish troubles, the coal-mines dispute, the engagement of the Princess Royal, and the murder of Irene Wilkins at Bournemouth. Locally there was little outstanding news, apart from the opening of the Westham Bridge at Weymouth.

Competition between the two Dorset evening papers was very keen, but, despite the many advantages the *Daily Press* enjoyed as a result of being printed in Weymouth, the *Echo* steadily gained support and prestige, so much so that at the beginning of 1924 the *Press* ceased publication. The directors of the Hampshire Advertiser Company were magnanimous in victory; having acquired the copyright, goodwill, offices and plant of their Dorset opponent, they took over the staff as well. On January 7, 1924, the *Echo* was for the first time printed in Weymouth – on the presses of its now defunct rival.

News was now received by private wire from the Fleet

Street headquarters of the world's greatest news-gathering agencies, the Press Association and Reuters (of which the Company had for many years been a subscribing member), and with three daily editions the *Echo* was able to give Dorset complete coverage of local, national and foreign events and happenings. At the annual meeting in 1924 the shareholders were told: "During the past year the directors acquired the Dorset Daily Press Limited at Weymouth, including their premises, 57 and 58 St. Thomas Street, and their plant and machinery, with the result that the *Dorset Daily Echo* is now the only daily newspaper circulating in that area."

Circulation and demand for advertising space grew rapidly and the old, dilapidated offices of the *Dorset Press* ("the ramshackle, rat-ridden premises in which the opposition paper had been produced", to quote one member of the staff at that time) were pulled down and replaced by an up-to-date newspaper plant. The Company's report for the year 1925 merely states: "the premises at 57 and 58 St. Thomas Street, Weymouth, have been rebuilt, and the old premises at 2 St. Mary Street, Weymouth, satisfactorily disposed of". Behind this terse statement lay a dramatic transformation act. Rebuilding was started and completed within a few months. The attractive modern office (*Echo* Chambers) which replaced the old bow-fronted shop premises consisted of a spacious front office and manager's office on the ground floor, editorial department on the first floor, and cashier's office and stores on the second.

Two men who did outstanding work in consolidating the success of the *Dorset Echo* in those early years were Mr. George Stephens and Mr. C. F. Carr. Mr. Stephens was the paper's first Manager and Mr. Carr its first Editor. In May, 1924, the Company recognised the latter's unusual combination of business acumen and editorial flair by transferring him to Southampton as Assistant Manager and Assistant Editor at headquarters. Later he was to become Editor of the *Southern Echo* and General Manager of the Company during a crucial period of its history.

CHAPTER II

Progress in the 30s

DURING THIS PERIOD, growth was also taking place in other parts of the Company's territory. In 1921 premises in Old Christchurch Road, Bournemouth, were acquired and adapted for the *Bournemouth Echo*. At about the same time a Salisbury branch was opened, and in the following year offices were opened in Winchester. In 1925 – to quote the report of that year – "a commodious garage and mess-rooms were erected in Spa Road, Southampton, and the facilities afforded by the latter for rest, refreshment and recreation are much appreciated by the staff of the Southampton office". (Incidentally, when this garage-social hall block is replaced in 1967 the last phase of the Company's present post-war rebuilding programme at Southampton will have been completed.)

The year 1924 saw important changes in the management of the Company. Mr. Goldsmith retired from the position of General Manager, having successfully guided the firm's activities through years of great difficulty as well as of expansion, and was succeeded by his deputy, Mr. W. A. Gleave. Captain A. E. Jones, M.C., then became Editor of the *Southern Echo* and Deputy General Manager of the Company.

Gleave and Jones – surely there has never been a more successful combination in the history of provincial journalism! Both had entered the newspaper game by way of sports reporting; both were men who combined in an unusual degree journalistic talent with executive ability; both had a gift for friendship. Yet temperamentally they were opposites. "Billy" Gleave, as we have seen, was jovial, easy-going (except on those rare occasions when firmness was required) and the most approachable of bosses. "Jonah" – as Captain Jones was affectionately known – never quite lost the military manner which, with his easily stirred Welsh fire, made him seem a somewhat formidable personality to junior members of the staff. (Who, having experienced it, will never forget the way he presided over the production of the *Football Echo* each Saturday afternoon throughout the season, as though it were a military operation!)

It is no exaggeration to say that "Billy" was one of the most popular men in Southampton during the long period in which he edited the *Southern Echo* and then managed the affairs of the Company. His many friends, drawn from all walks of life, admired not only his genial disposition, but his fine personal qualities. He was a brilliant raconteur, a widely read man, a deep student of human nature. One who knew him well wrote of him: "His experience as a journalist and later as a magistrate impressed him particularly with the fact that there are always two sides to a question, and whenever asked for his opinion, as he often was on a variety of subjects, he never gave it lightly, and always suspended judgment until he was in possession of all the facts. He was a Bohemian, and one of the rapidly diminishing circle of old-time journalists who possessed not only ability, but outstanding personality. Yet, allied to personal charm, he had a very shrewd business mind which became particularly evident after his appointment to the responsible post of General Manager. . . . Not only did his manifold capabilities impress themselves upon local public life, but in the course of years he established for himself a very high reputation in journalistic circles throughout the country. He was indeed a national figure in his profession. . . ."

Mr. Gleave was naturally very proud of the good relations which existed between management and staff, and he derived immense satisfaction from the fact that the General Strike in 1926 failed to stop the Company's presses. What astonished him was that any of the employees should have wanted to down tools.

As he wrote in *Echograms*, the Company's house journal: "We had all heard the distant rumblings of industrial unrest, but few of us, I imagine, thought that we as a firm would be involved in the cataclysm which ensued. But we were; and that was a very amazing thing to me, for I was unaware that any member of our staffs had any grievance, and newspapers, as a rule, are undisturbed by outside considerations.

"Even if a General Strike were called, we, at any rate, expected to publish as usual. We did so, but with sadly depleted staffs. Especially was this the case at Bournemouth. All credit, therefore, to those who remained steadfast. But what of those who failed us? I believe – and I hope I am correct in the belief – that most of the latter were grievously misled, and doubtless regret, as much as I deplore, their ill-considered action. This, however, is no time for useless recriminations. Although, metaphorically speaking, the strikers banged the doors behind them when they ceased work on the night of May 3, they found the portals open wide when they returned to work the following week. That, at any rate, should serve to show that the directors and management harboured no ill-feeling. We have all learned a lesson. I trust therefore that there will be a general disposition to forget, as far as possible, the past. What has been done cannot be undone, so let us look hopefully to the future."

The strike halted publication of many papers throughout the country, but all three of the firm's evenings were on the streets every day of the dispute – greatly reduced in size, of course, but carrying all the news about the strike, both national and local. This was the first time that the *Echos* used the "new-fangled" wireless to obtain information. At Weymouth members of the staff clambered on to the roof to erect an aerial and reporters took shorthand notes of every bulletin issued throughout the day.

Mr. R. R. Gleave, the present General Manager, recalls that no sooner had the national newspapers ceased to come out than official representations were made to the Company, asking for its assistance in the production of the *British Gazette*, a small tabloid which was being published by the Government to allay panic and give the public essential information. Several distinguished personages from Whitehall arrived at the Westwood Road home of Mr. W. A. Gleave at around midnight and after lengthy talks it was agreed that Mr. T. Walcroft, the Company's superintendent engineer, should be released from his normal duties and attached to the staff of the *British Gazette* while the strike lasted. The Company also helped a Channel Islands daily to keep going by lending it one or two skilled men from the *Southern Echo*.

It was the General Strike which brought about the first big change in the appearance of the *Dorset Echo*. Because of the shortage of news and advertising and the difficulty of typesetting, it was impossible to maintain the large page, and a tabloid style was substituted. The smaller page was so successful that when the strike ended it was decided to continue with the "emergency" format, and during World War II the *Bournemouth* and *Southern Echos* also adopted this more convenient tabloid size.

In 1926 the Company bought the Palace Theatre, together with the York Yard behind it, adjoining their premises in Above Bar. The Yard was wanted to provide space for an extension to the works; the Palace site for possible expansion in the future. Later in the year the new building was completed, and on July 30, 1927, the Rt. Hon. Wilfred Ashley, M.P., Minister of Transport, performed the opening ceremony and started the new rotary presses. At an extraordinary general meeting of the shareholders that autumn the Company's title was changed to "Southern Newspapers Limited". ("Hampshire Advertiser and Echos Limited" had been a short-lived compromise.)

In 1928 the directors reported "with deep regret the loss by death of their valued colleague, Mr. J. C. Moberly, who had been a director of the Company since 1914".

Mr. Moberly was the doyen of Southampton lawyers, having

been admitted a solicitor in 1872. Member of a well-known Wessex family – his father was George Moberly, for thirty-one years Headmaster of Winchester College and then Bishop of Salisbury – he took a prominent part in the business life of Southampton and the ecclesiastical affairs of the Winchester Diocese. His place on the board was taken by Mr. W. A. Gleave.

During the years of post-war trade depression, Southampton suffered less than did many of the nation's ports and industrial towns. The fact that the port depended more on passenger than cargo traffic made all the difference. While hundreds of thousands of tons of freight shipping were laid up on the Mersey, the Thames and the Humber, there was a constant movement of great passenger liners up and down Southampton Water. In 1919 the Cunard Steamship Company decided to make the Docks the terminus of their New York services, and soon its largest vessels – the *Mauretania*, the *Aquitania* and the *Berengaria* – were using the port. By 1924 Southampton's post-war recovery was well under way and in that year the Prince of Wales (now Duke of Windsor) came to the town to open the world's largest floating dry dock, and an Act of Parliament was passed authorising the Southern Railway to spend £13 million on a vast scheme to reclaim 460 acres of mudland from the River Test and extend the docks frontage for two miles.

The Editor of the *Southern Echo*, Captain Jones, played a key role, albeit an unofficial one, in the negotiations between the railway company, the local authority and the landowners which preceded work on the docks extension scheme. During a period when secrecy was essential, he acted as liaison officer, keeping contact between Colonel G. S. Szlumper, the Docks and Marine Manager at that time, and the Corporation. When the negotiations were brought to a successful conclusion Captain Jones's reward was an exclusive story for his paper – the *Echo*'s biggest scoop. The part which he played in these events was not revealed until many years later, when

Southampton Chamber of Commerce took the unusual step of making him an Honorary Member in recognition of his valuable services to the commercial community.

The work on the new docks was carried out between 1927 and 1934, and included one and a half miles of quays, a number of large transit sheds and passenger reception buildings, and a dry dock capable of accommodating any ship afloat, which King George V opened in 1933.

A member of the editorial staff whose typewriter must have been working overtime in those days was Mr. R. R. Gleave, the shipping reporter (later Shipping Editor), who was destined to become General Manager of the Company in 1957. For those were the years when Southampton Docks produced more good news stories than any place in the country outside London. And Mr. Gleave – "Reg" to his colleagues – not only interviewed all the celebrities passing through, but also recorded the daily life of the waterfront in his "Round the Port" column and in the special articles which he wrote for the *Echo* and the *Hampshire Advertiser*.

Before returning to what is strictly Company history, perhaps it would be of interest to take another glance at Southampton's progress during the 30s. The relative prosperity of the Docks was reflected in the great civic developments which occurred during this time. These included the building of a Civic Centre (municipal offices, law courts, guildhall, library and art gallery), the laying out of well-planned Corporation housing estates, and the growth of the University College, which in time was to become the University of Southampton.

As I wrote in *Collected Essays on Southampton*, the town now possessed not only a worthy headquarters for all its administrators and civic governors, but also a cultural centre well equipped to stimulate interest in music and the arts. New schools and churches arose to keep pace with the needs of a growing population, and with the building of the Empire (now the Gaumont) Southampton possessed one of the largest theatres in the country, where West End productions of drama, ballet and opera could be seen.

By 1934 the docks traffic was back to the pre-depression level, and in that year the Cunard and White Star Lines joined forces. On May 27, 1936, the *Queen Mary* – then the world's largest vessel – sailed on her maiden voyage from Southampton to New York in an atmosphere of excitement and optimism. But as the 30s drew to a close the dark shadows of world events fell across Southampton. Ships began to arrive laden with refugee children from Spain . . . and the Corporation began to organise a Civil Defence Department.

Turning again to domestic affairs, we find that in 1932 important changes took place in the Company's directorate. Ill-health caused Mr. W. Frank Perkins, Chairman since 1901, to retire from the board. The vacancy was filled by his eldest son, Mr. W. R. D. Perkins, M.P. (Sir Robert Perkins, the present Chairman), and he was succeeded as Chairman by his brother-in-law, Sir Russell Bencraft. Another member of the Perkins family, Colonel Sir Edwin Perkins – a former M.P. for Southampton – was elected Deputy Chairman.

During the years of his retirement Mr. W. Frank Perkins, who died in 1946, devoted himself to his lifelong interests: farming and the history of agriculture and the New Forest. His bibliographies on these subjects are standard works, and his unique library of over 2,000 agricultural books is now a prized possession of Southampton University.

In 1932 changes also occurred in the management at Bournemouth. Mr. H. J. Cheverton, who had been Manager of the *Bournemouth Echo* for twenty-one years, retired, and was succeeded by his deputy, Mr. Robert Fairbairn. Mr. Douglas Alan Gleave, second son of Mr. W. A. Gleave, who had gained a wide experience of newspaper advertising in the Southampton and London offices of the Company, was appointed Assistant Manager.

The biggest change of all in the history of the *Bournemouth Echo* was marked by the opening, on January 26, 1934, of its

new premises on Richmond Hill. The ceremony was performed by Lord Mottistone (Jack Seely), the Lord Lieutenant
of the county. Designed on modern functional lines, this
building held its place for a good many years as the most
contemporary-looking newspaper office in the provinces. And
not surprisingly its erection during a period of trade depression
caused both puzzlement and admiration. As the *Bournemouth
Echo* itself said in the special souvenir issue which marked the
occasion:

"To most thinking people the marvel will not be that a
newspaper should create for itself a bigger home, and pardon-
ably seek the prominence of gleaming walls facing four sides
of the compass to house every modern appliance in newspaper
production – the marvel is that such a conception should have
coincided with the worst period in the country's economic
history, and that it should have been embarked upon when
retrenchment and restriction were the mottoes prevailing in
industry. . . .

"The *Echo*, in the format to which the present generation has
become accustomed, could well have served until the turn of
the tide towards national recovery denoted a safer passage for
the launching of such a venture. Nor were considerations such
as the falling in of leases to dictate any change. The *Echo*
owned its own premises, and continuous improvements in their
structure had permitted all known needs to be met – but just
for the present.

"A mere policy of 'safety first' as an excuse for retarding
natural expansion would, however, have been another gesture
of despondency. . . . The need nationally and locally was a
display of bold enterprise as one of the surest means of re-
establishing confidence. That 'tide in the affairs of men' which,
in the Shakespearian philosophy, 'leads on to fortune', pre-
supposes that ventures are to be ready for the launching if they
hope to 'take the current when it serves'."

Naturally, the opening of the new office at Bournemouth
recalled memories of the first day in the life of the paper. These

were recorded by the late Mr. W. A. Park, who was Editor from 1900 to 1947:

"Technicalities would bore the reader, but an outline showing how meagre and humble was our birth place might give some idea of the early conditions under which we worked. It was an empty hall in Holdenhurst Road, opposite the East Cliff Congregational Church. In one corner a partition formed a reporters' room, with enough space to contain a table for four. Another such cabin adjoined it for two Linotype machines. In the opposite corner a space was partitioned off for the Manager, and a continuance of this screen made an enclosure for paper storage on the inner side, and on the outer was a long trestle table on which the papers were counted and made into parcels for delivery. This job called for muscular alertness and so the packers were reinforced by a young lady whose skill with the paste brush and her sergeant-major methods with over-eager news-boys earned her the title of 'Princess Paste'.

"The printing machine – a single-decker – and its equipment were installed near the middle of the hall, leaving down the centre an aisle wide enough to provide a pitch for a dinner-hour game of cricket with a paper ball. Stretching across the bottom of the hall was a concert platform, utilised during the midday break by a Salvation Army bandsman for practising on a cornet. Sometimes those who 'stayed in' to dinner would hear one of the compositors roundly berating an apprentice for some prank, to a musical background of the soothing 'Voice that breathed o'er Eden' from the concert platform.

"When our third reporter arrived – a lad led in by his clerical father – we had to send out to borrow a soap-box for use as a chair for him. The boy had a liking for sport, and from sports reporter rose to be Sports Editor, remaining so until the outbreak of the First World War.

"Apart from the importance of the event, the launching of the paper is memorable to me on account of an amusing hitch that occurred right at the outset. For this first publication, the printing press was started by the then Mayor, Alderman J. C.

Webber, known to his friends as 'Honest John', who, except when the occasion forbade, was rarely seen without a cigar in his mouth. We used to have bets about that cigar. If he put it down while he went for his innings at a cricket match, or when he was called from a circle of friends to conduct some brief business, wagers were at once made that the cigar would still be alight when he returned. In the majority of instances it was.

"In his mayoral robes, Alderman Webber stood by to pull the lever that would start the press. The last adjustments were being made when down went the cigar, the Mayor having taken as his cue a shout from one of the machine-men. He pulled the lever, and as the first copies came off it was discovered that one of the inside pages was being printed upside down!"

★   ★   ★

In 1936 Colonel Sir Edwin Perkins, who had served as a director since 1914, retired through ill-health, and Mr. Harry Parsons, head of a well-known Southampton marine engineering company, was elected to fill the vacancy. Because of the growth of the Company's activities, Colonel G. F. Perkins, D.S.O., was elected at this time as an additional director.

In 1937 a process department was opened at the Bournemouth office, thus completing the ambitious rebuilding scheme planned at the beginning of the decade. No one realised it at the time, of course, but the new office at Bournemouth was to save the life of the Company, for in the war which was drawing near Southern Newspapers were to lose their premises in both Southampton and Weymouth.

CHAPTER 12

When the Bombs Fell

THE LATE Bernard Knowles, in his war history of the southern port,[1] describes Southampton as a frontier town. And, with the French coast less than 100 miles away, the description is an apt one. During the Middle Ages this proximity to France was a source of constant danger, which the citizens tried to avert by fortifying their town with stout walls and battlemented towers.

Gunpowder long ago made such precautions useless, and with the coming of the aeroplane every town in Britain was exposed to bombardment. But Southampton's geographical position and strategical importance increased its vulnerability, and, not surprisingly, the local authority was one of the first in England to take air-raid precautions seriously. During the month preceding the outbreak of war in 1939, 100 basement shelters – for the most part medieval wine cellars strengthened and adapted for the purpose – were opened in the older part of the town, providing accommodation for 10,000 people. There was no thirteenth-century vault or undercroft near the *Echo* office, so the Company had a reinforced concrete shelter constructed under the paper store at the rear of their Above Bar premises. Here Linotype machines were set up, so that the production of the newspaper could continue during raids.

Events were now rapidly leading towards the disaster which had been threatening Europe and the whole world ever since Adolf Hitler and his Nazis had obtained power in Germany six years previously. "On August 26", writes Knowles, "teachers

---

[1] *Southampton – the English Gateway* (Hutchinson).

and schoolchildren in the town were abruptly recalled from vacation. Two days later the evacuation scheme was fully rehearsed. On August 30 Southampton docks became a closed area to all except those having business there. That same day the *Queen Mary* . . . left Southampton for New York. When she passed Bishop's Rock she passed out of sight and almost out of knowledge of her home port for five and a half years. On August 30, too, A.R.P. headquarters ominously announced that from that date the sirens would not be sounded except in the event of an actual air-raid. Two days later a still grimmer note was struck. On September 1 and 2 thousands of the youth population were evacuated. They were accompanied by expectant mothers, the blind, the crippled, teachers and registered helpers. . . ."

For one of the reporters who covered the great evacuation, it was impossible to remain unmoved "as childish footsteps echoed along Manor Farm Road this gloomy September morning to herald Southampton's first evacuation assembly. Children of all ages sat in the brilliantly-lit classrooms. Some of the toddlers were not properly awake. Others, a bit older, were playing about, blissfully unaware of what was happening." The authorities were reported as being disappointed over the number of parents who had withdrawn their children from the scheme at the last minute. The horrors of modern warfare were still not generally realised, in spite of all that had been written on the subject.

In the special edition which the *Echo* published on Sunday, September 3, a leading article urged its readers to be of good courage. "So it is war at last", began the editorial. "Germany has made the fateful choice and has plunged Europe into a conflict that threatens the very existence of civilisation. Whatever blood is spilt will be upon her head. We at least enter this grim struggle with a clear conscience. We have tried every means to avoid it. We have seen Nazi Germany gradually devouring European peoples who could not resist, and for the sake of peace we have held our hand. But there has always been a limit. That limit has now been reached. . . . Sacrifice will be demanded of all. It will be made willingly, with faith in the cause for which we are fighting and in the strength of our arms, but above all in God the Almighty Ruler and Disposer of events, to whom we humbly pray for help, courage, guidance and, if it be His will, victory!"

An *Echo* feature-writer compared the contemporary situation to that of the Dark Ages and found encouragement in the lessons of history and the faith displayed by men in times past. "How hopeless, how desolate Europe must have seemed as the sixth century dawned",[1] he wrote. "In our part of the world the once noble cities of Winchester, Portchester and Silchester, with their paved streets, their villas, their shops, their public baths and their Christian basilicas, were waste lands. . . . But already another dawn was at hand. Europe was conquered again, but by the Christian gospel of love. From Ireland, from Italy, little bands of men, who carried no weapons except their faith and goodness, set out to bring civilisation and religion back to the peoples of Europe."

To be candid, however, that was not quite the spirit in which Southampton faced the grim realities of the time. When war breaks out, long views become both difficult and unpopular. For most people the demands of the present moment are all-absorbing. The general fear and expectation in Southampton was that the town and port would suffer severe aerial assault within hours of war being declared. Hence the evacuation of thousands of schoolchildren to the comparative safety of the countryside, the preparations for dealing with heavy casualties, and the elaborate civil defence plans. But a full year was to elapse before air attacks on a serious scale took place – a year in which a British Expeditionary Force left Southampton Docks for France and in which pathetic remnants of that army limped back into the southern port after the evacuation from Dunkirk. During the period September, 1939, to June, 1940, nearly

[1] From "A Hampshire Scrapbook", appearing in "Topics of the Hour", the *Southern Echo*'s gossip feature.

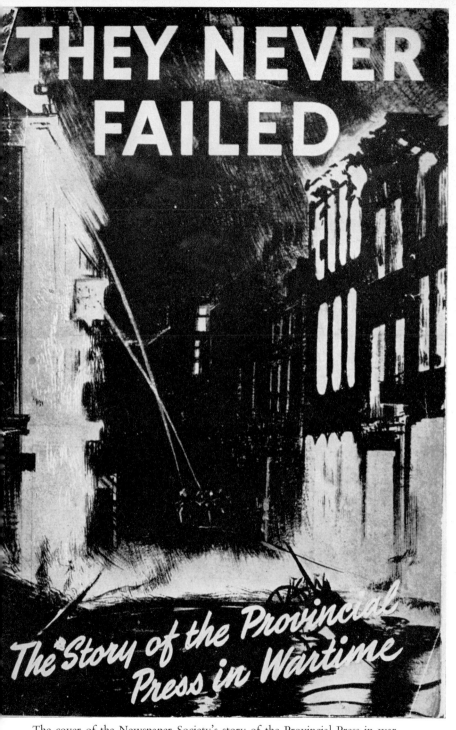

THEY NEVER FAILED

FAILED

The Story of the Provincial Press in Wartime

The cover of the Newspaper Society's story of the Provincial Press in war-
time, which recounts the reverses sustained by Southern Newspapers Limited
during the years of conflict. (Two of the Company's offices were destroyed by
enemy action.)

This was what the composing room at Southampton looked like after the great blitz.

Above: This was the pre-war scene in Above Bar as seen from the *Echo* office windows.

Below: The same street after central Southampton had been destroyed by Nazi bombs.

Demolition in progress at the *Dorset Echo* office and works, after the building had been destroyed in an air-raid on April 2, 1942.

600,000 troops left the Docks and almost 200,000 disembarked.

After the fall of France came the Battle of Britain, in which Southampton played a key role. The famous Spitfire fighter had been designed by a local man – the late R. J. Mitchell – and up to June, 1940, the production of Spitfires was confined solely to the Southampton works of the Vickers-Supermarine Company. (In August of that year the Mayor opened a Spitfire Fund as a memorial to Mitchell.)

The air-raids on the town began at this time, but production was maintained, despite constant air-raid alarms. In this connection, Mr. Palmer recalls preparing dividend warrants in the shelter under the paper store (already referred to) in 1940 while the floor shuddered with the concussion of bombs. The raids reached a peak of intensity on the nights of November 30 and December 1, when the commercial centre of Southampton was destroyed by fire-bombs. The *Echo* office was gutted, all that remained being charred debris, twisted girders and – miraculously – the press room at the back of the building.

This was how Mr. Geoffrey O'Connor (Patoc), then chief reporter of the *Southern Echo*, remembers that terrible week-end:

"Saturday, November 30, 1940, had darkened into a cold, crisp night when the air-raid sirens moaned in dismal chorus. Scarcely had the wailing faded when the sky above Southampton began to change colour. Between the blacked-out town and the German raiders, droning high at first, then daringly low, there glided down, slowly, ominously and ever brighter the parachute flares that picked out the Luftwaffe's target for the night. Soon the flares were countless. They shed a merciless glare on a town that was within the next six hours to rock and tremble and become a blazing mass, the glare of which could be seen as far away as Weymouth. Southern Newspapers' headquarters in Above Bar was but one of the bigger places destroyed that night. Before the merciful dawn of Sunday, emergency arrangements, made as soon as the war started, were put into operation. Under this elaborate plan,

H

with which every *Echo* worker was familiar, the *Southern Echo* immediately began to move to Bournemouth to complete preparations to publish Monday's editions on the plant of one of the sister journals, the *Bournemouth Echo*. Sub-editors and telegraphists, compositors, foundry-men, press-minders and most of those concerned with the making of the *Southern Echo* left the shambles of Southampton for the orderliness and peace of, then, unattacked Bournemouth.

"Reporters stayed on to gather and tell the story of Southampton's blitz – or as much of it as strict censorship allowed. Also left in Southampton were the advertising staff and clerical staff. . . . News was kept flowing by a relay of motor-cyclists, who made hourly dashes to Winchester and, after long delays on the congested lines, telephoned copy to Bournemouth from there. And so it was that while hundreds of buildings were still burning or smouldering, and while rescue squads were still digging in the ruins to release the injured and recover the bodies of the many who had died, the *Southern Daily Echo* appeared as usual early on Monday afternoon. . . ."

★   ★   ★

Mr. B. D. Knowles, who was Secretary of the Chamber of Commerce at that time, relates how firemen, exhausted but still battling with fires in Cumberland Place, raised a rousing cheer as the first *Echo* delivery van pulled up outside the Chamber offices, in which the editorial staff had found a temporary home. Under the title "Southampton Lives" that night's leading article ran:

"Southampton has endured a great ordeal. With London, with Coventry and Birmingham, its citizens have faced the fury and horror of German terror raiders. We know now the worst that a relentless enemy can do to us and although our streets are scarred, the town still lives. Even as we survey with sorrowful hearts the evil work, we know that Southampton, with a past of over 1,000 years, can look forward to a great future. Although the barbarism of the twentieth century is worse than anything experienced in past ages, we Southern English, who have long memories, do not forget that more than once our port has suffered at the hands of enemies and has risen again. While the lessons of history may offer us some consolation, we would do well, at a time like this, to look to the future. We, the people of Southampton, the people of Britain, are fighting for a world in which there will be no Luftwaffes, no nightly sirens, no terror that flieth by night. We shall build anew, not only our houses and shops and our public buildings, but our social order. Hitler's 'New Order', ushered in to the accompaniment of the scream of bombs and the crackle of destructive fire, is as old as human cruelty and tyranny. Our aim is a free world of free men and women. In such a world Southampton will once again become the Gateway to Britain, the great port from which ships and planes, merchandise and travellers, will reach out to all corners of the world. Meanwhile, we do not by any means consider ourselves in the past tense. Thank God the overwhelming majority of our citizens – the real Southampton – survive today, amazingly cheerful, full of courage, not lacking in hope."

★   ★   ★

For a more detailed account of what happened to the headquarters of the Company on the night of November 30 we have the report of Captain A. E. Jones, M.C., Deputy General Manager and Editor of the *Southern Echo*:

"I regret to have to report that during a severe enemy air-raid on the night of Saturday, November 30, our offices and works at Above Bar were almost entirely destroyed by fire. A. Sheriff, our fire-watcher, assisted by other members of the staff who were sleeping in the Company's air-raid shelter, extinguished four incendiary bombs that fell on the premises, and might have prevented the conflagration that ensued had not the water supply failed. As it was, the whole of the editorial and commercial offices, as well as the news composing room, process department and jobbing machine room were gutted out but, most fortunately, the stereotyping foundry, press-room and publishing room were only slightly damaged. The effect of the fire made it impossible to continue to print the *Southern Daily Echo* at Southampton; but, thanks to arrangements that had been made previously with our Bournemouth Office to meet such an emergency, there was no interruption in the publication of the paper."

★   ★   ★

Here Mr. W. A. Gleave, J.P., General Manager and Editor-in-chief, takes up the story in a special report to the board:

"To enable this to be done, fine staff work was accomplished by Captain Jones, Mr. Carr,[1] Mr. Baker,[2] Mr. Hoskin, composing department, Mr. House, publishing, and others.

"During the next three weeks, the whole staff worked under the most difficult conditions. Temporary accommodation had to be sought in every available direction. The Principal of the Gregg School placed at our disposal such facilities as he could afford, with the result that as time went on we found ourselves occupying three rooms, with the use of seven typewriters – three for reporters, two for typists and two for the advertisement department. Furthermore, we were provided with paper, pens, pencils, ink, carbons, envelopes, etc. Mr. Bernard Knowles, Secretary of the Southampton Chamber of Commerce, kindly invited me to share his office, and placed at our disposal basement accommodation for the reception of small advertisements. Everyone was, indeed, most kind and considerate. The public were not slow to express their appreciation of our unbroken continuance of publication. Our first issue was a very small one – only four pages – but on the second day we increased to eight, and on the third to twelve. Advertisements

[1] C. F. Carr, then Assistant Editor and Assistant Manager of the *Southern Echo*.

[2] R. E. Baker, then Advertisement Manager of the *Southern Echo*, later Advertisement Manager-in-chief of the Company. His immediate predecessor was Mr. F. George, who had been Southampton Manager of the National Telephone Company before his appointment as Advertisement Manager of the *Echo*.

continued to pour in, and before the end of the week we published a sixteen-page paper and the circulation had grown from 35,000 on Monday to 37,000 on Saturday. Next week it rose to 40,000 or only 5,000 less than our usual winter figures. This was made possible by the loyal co-operation of the Bournemouth Manager and his staff.

"For the first few days we had to contend with the dislocation of our Creed telegraphic system, but, thanks to the leviathan efforts of our Postmaster, Mr. Alfred Bell, the trouble was rectified within a few days. Meantime, our working staff strove to clear up the mess amidst the ruins of the old office, salvaging much melted metal which had percolated from the upper floors, and which hung like silvery stalactites in the candle-light. Such virgin metal as was recovered was sent to Bournemouth, and the residuum to the metal-founders for refinement. But in such a ghastly setting little could be done, and at the end of the year nothing remained to be recovered – nothing but twisted girders and gnarled Linotype machines.

"Following this disaster", Mr. Gleave continued, "I received scores of letters expressing sympathy and offering such assistance as could be rendered. First on the scene was Mr. Bert Chivers of Devizes, a well-known Wiltshire contractor (and incidentally a shareholder), volunteering his services in any way. Some necessary demolition has since been accomplished, but much remains to be done in the way of site clearing. His difficulty may be shortage of labour.

"The late Mr. Jack Baker was the supervisor of our inventory, so I got into touch as soon as possible with his former right-hand man, Mr. Livingstone, who actually compiled it, and at an informal meeting of the board he was instructed to present our case for war claims. A first-class man, he lost no time in setting about the business and, as far as stock is concerned, he has already succeeded in obtaining for us a sum in the region of £4,000 for lost paper, in the Spa Road store and the jobbing department. Claims for stores are acknowledged immediately, but not so with plant. As regards the latter, we may have to wait until the war is over. The claim will be substantial, inasmuch as we lost seventeen Linotype machines, two Monotype machines, and an expensive American Ludlow type-casting machine. These, together with other lost plant, should at least realise £10,000. As regards the jobbing and news composing and process plants, there is no question of salvage – all is lost. We were fortunate, however, to preserve our rotary printing presses and foundry. Mr. Livingstone would have claimed all of £11,500 for each of our printing presses, although not of modern type, and our foundry plant (happily spared) was worth not less than £6,000. So much to the good. Things might have been worse."

The destruction was not confined to the buildings and plant. The greater portion of the Company's records were lost, including the whole of the contents of the board room, containing the Secretary's minute books and other files going back to the inception of the Company. The safe containing these fell from top to bottom of the building and burst open. The contents were entirely destroyed. Several files of the early editions of the Company's newspaper were also burned.

Fortunately, the private ledger, share register and some minute books were stored elsewhere and these vital documents were thus saved. The major financial and secretarial records of the Company had to be entirely reconstructed from such evidence as was available. This was the task of Mr. R. I. Palmer, then Assistant Secretary, whose comment was: "It is surprising what we can do without."

The sales ledgers were charred, but legible, and Mr. E. S. Fuidge, the Chief Accountant, was able to reconstitute them and thus collect all moneys due!

★   ★   ★

The story of the Company during the Second World War is related at some length in a Newspaper Society publication, *They Never Failed*, dealing with the wartime record of the

English Provincial Press. After remarking that Southern Newspapers Limited probably suffered the heaviest loss of any newspaper undertaking in the country as the result of enemy action, it says:

"Almost complete destruction of the head office and works at Southampton . . . was followed by destruction of the *Dorset Daily Echo* offices at Weymouth on April 3, 1942. Despite this, not a single day's publication of any of the company's three daily newspapers was missed. These two disasters threw a severe strain on the company's remaining equipment at Bournemouth, and also on the staffs, which had been greatly depleted by Service requirements. Fortunately, the premises and plant at Bournemouth were modern, the building having been completed only a few years before the outbreak of war. For thirteen months this one office, designed for the production of one paper, produced three evening papers serving that South Coast area.

"Before all this happened, the *Echo* works at Southampton had a narrow escape when, on November 6, 1940, six fighter-bombers which were attacked over the town jettisoned their bombs. They dropped 12 H.E.s in pairs, and most of them fell in the centre of the town. Houses in Portland Street were wrecked, and one of the bombs tore its way into the earth alongside the *Echo* press room, but failed to explode. It was not known whether it was a delayed-action bomb or a dud. Although there was a danger that the vibration of the big rotary presses would make it explode, the machine-room crews volunteered to carry on and produce the usual editions. Meanwhile, their colleagues from the works were helping to dig out the buried victims of the Portland Street bombs. The bomb outside the works did not explode, and on the same evening it was extricated and taken away by a bomb-disposal squad.

"During one of the worst of Southampton's many raids, the Above Bar offices and works were gutted. . . . Early in the evening fire-bombs came down in showers, and the *Echo* offices and works were among the first buildings to be set on fire. The firm's fire-guards did their best, but the blaze was soon out of control. The firemen were early hampered by lack of water, mains having been smashed. The adjoining Palace Theatre was on fire, and there was little that anybody could do. When the flames died down it was seen that, except for the press room at the back of the building, the offices and works were a ruin. . . . The wreckage smouldered for weeks, and when it was eventually possible to remove the debris and open the strong-room in which the files of the company's newspapers were kept it was found that the intense heat had charred many of the volumes, which covered more than a century of local newspaper records.

"Emergency arrangements which had been made early in the war were immediately put into effect and the majority of the staff were transferred to Bournemouth, thirty miles away, where they set about the task of producing the first of many editions of the *Southern Daily Echo* to be printed on the companion journal's presses. The transfer took place on a Sunday. On the following Monday the *Southern Daily Echo* was on sale in battered and still burning Southampton half an hour *earlier* than usual! . . . When the first van brought back the *Echo* from Bournemouth, firemen who were dealing with a blaze at the Trojans' Club raised a cheer and greeted the driver with 'Good old *Echo*!' A few seconds later they were grasping hoses with one hand and holding a copy of the *Echo* in the other. The people of Southampton showed keen appreciation of the maintenance of continuity; they looked upon the appearance of their evening paper as usual as an earnest of the town's determination to surmount the tragedy which had befallen it. The Bishop of Winchester, Dr. Garbett, later Archbishop of York, was among the first to call upon the management and congratulate them upon keeping going.

"In 1942 Southern Newspapers received a second blow. Early on the morning of Good Friday, executives were called out of bed to be told that the *Dorset Daily Echo* works at

Weymouth had been destroyed. This was a particularly unlucky blow for the company, as the bomb which wrecked the works in the Dorset town was the only one that fell among the business premises in that raid. Only a few hours before the bomb fell, expensive new plant had been installed in the foundry. The youngest of the group of three evening papers was forced to join the other two at Bournemouth and share the *Bournemouth Daily Echo*'s presses.

"For two and a half years, until small temporary premises could be built on the Above Bar site, the *Southern Daily Echo* transport had to travel sixty miles a day before delivering a single copy of the paper, and it has been estimated that during that period the fleet of delivery vans covered not less than 393,750 miles. This was in all sorts of circumstances, but throughout the two and a half years the *Echo* was never more than a few minutes late in reaching Southampton and other towns in the circulation area than when production was possible in Southampton itself. All manner of emergency arrangements had to be carried out to maintain production. . . . When the Weymouth office was destroyed copy was being set in the Bournemouth office for the eight-page paper while members of the Weymouth staff were busy salvaging anything that could be saved from the wreckage of the works there. There was a touch of irony about the discovery at Weymouth that the only type standing after the blitz was a tied-up display advertisement with the heading 'Hitler's Nightmare!'

"The Bournemouth plant had bombs all around it, but came through unscathed. Soon after the destruction of the Southampton works, the company was faced with the necessity of guarding against further emergencies, and at one period no fewer than eight carefully planned and highly detailed emergency schemes existed on paper ready for immediate operation if the necessity arose. These plans included the appointment of billeting officers, whose job it would have been to proceed to various production points to arrange accommodation for the large staffs which would have had to be removed at a moment's notice. Arrangements were also made for radio transmission of news to emergency production points to safeguard against the failure of the telegraph and telephone systems. With two of its three printing offices destroyed, Southern Newspapers Limited kept faith with the public and published without break its three evening newspapers.''

CHAPTER 13

Soldiering On

BY MARCH, 1941, four Linotype machines salvaged from Southampton had been set up in the Bournemouth works, thus enabling the Southampton composing staff to act as a self-contained unit. It was now possible to produce only one edition of the *Southern Echo* each day. That spring bombs fell within 100 yards of the Bournemouth office on two occasions, so it was thought advisable to plan alternative arrangements in the event of serious damage to the plant. (The *Bournemouth Echo* was to be printed at Weymouth, and the *Southern* on the presses of the *Evening News* in Portsmouth.)

In May the board learnt that the Southampton presses, which had survived the blitz, had been dismantled and that the site of the office and works had been cleared. The directors began at once to think seriously about rebuilding, but decided to wait for the town reconstruction plan before getting down to details. One thing was certain – the new headquarters would be larger than the old. Since there was no question of rebuilding the Palace Theatre, considerably more site space would be available.

Orders were placed for machinery, to be delivered when the war was over, and a first claim of £35,000 for plant damaged or destroyed by enemy action was made on behalf of the Company.

On three successive days during the summer of 1941 all three papers had to be produced without a line of Creed or telephone news, as a result of air raid damage in London.

B.B.C. radio bulletins and quotes from the national dailies helped to fill the columns normally devoted to agency messages. There were to be many occasions during the rest of the war when the Creed would be out of action for long periods and P.A.-Reuter reports would have to be phoned, but never again would telephone and telegraph be out of order at the same time.

The annual report for 1941 struck a note of typically British understatement. "The past year", it began, "has been one of considerable difficulty"!

When the shareholders met in September, the Chairman, Sir Russell Bencraft, expressed to them the board's pride in what had been achieved. "The fact that we were able to publish the *Southern Echo* the day following the big blitz," he said, "not only astonished the readers of that popular journal, but surprised the newspaper world, but not for the first time." He went on to recall that during the General Strike, Southern Newspapers Limited were almost alone in preserving continuity of publication.

What caused deep regret was news of the death of Mr. E. G. Burnett, Secretary of the Company for the previous thirty-four years, whose wise handling of its financial affairs had contributed greatly to its success during a period of unprecedented expansion. (Mr. J. P. Burnett, then serving in the Royal Navy, was appointed his successor, but at the end of the war decided not to take up the post, which was filled by Mr. R. I. Palmer, the Assistant Secretary, who had acted as Secretary during the difficult war years and who had been on Mr. E. G. Burnett's secretarial staff since 1923.) At the same meeting, the directors reported that Mr. Gleave, who had held the position of General Manager and Editor-in-chief since 1924, intended to retire at the end of the month. They were glad that he would continue to be a member of the board, and they "looked forward to the benefit of his wide experience and sound advice for many years to come".

The Company received its second great war-time blow on

April 2, 1942, when the offices of the *Dorset Echo* at Weymouth were destroyed in an air-raid. This is how the present Editor, Mr. Adlam, remembers the occasion:

"It was Maundy Thursday. New foundry equipment had been installed and was ready for production on Easter Saturday. The 'run' had been completed for four hours; all the readers had received their papers. The volunteer fire-watcher had been relieved by a professional just before 9 p.m., when a 'red' alert was operating. Then came the greatest test of all for the twenty-one-year-old *Dorset Echo*. Nazi dive-bombers swept in from over the sea, dropping bombs indiscriminately all over the town. Twenty people were killed in the raid and fifty-six seriously injured, and among the 'hits' was the *Echo* office. It was the only high-explosive bomb to fall in the shopping area of the town, and it exploded in the new foundry! The building was almost completely wrecked, but the fire-watcher escaped uninjured.

"Most of the staff met later that night, and plans were immediately made for salvaging what machinery and equipment was worth saving. And at the same time, the immediate future of the paper was decided. All the editorial staff were called to duty on Good Friday. Copy which had been lost had to be re-written and subbed and sent to Bournemouth, where *Dorset* joined the *Southern Echo* as 'guests' of the *Bournemouth Echo*. Composing room and machine room staffs were found accommodation in Bournemouth. In order to leave the machines free to produce the *Southern* and *Bournemouth Echos* as early as possible, the Editor (Mr. W. H. Hill) and one sub-editor began work each day at 7 a.m., after travelling by road from their homes in Weymouth.

"On Saturday, April 4, the *Dorset Echo* was on sale dead on time throughout the whole of its circulation area. With some modifications, this early arrangement was continued during the remaining seven years in which the paper was produced at Bournemouth, and, except when the roads were deep in snow, the edition was never more than a few minutes late."

On that memorable Saturday a twelve-pager was produced for Bournemouth and eight-pagers for Southampton and Weymouth. Press times were staggered as follows: *Southern Daily Echo*, 1.15 p.m. (41,200 copies); *Bournemouth Daily Echo* (country), 2.5 p.m. (2,400); *Dorset Daily Echo*, 2.10 p.m. (12,730); *Bournemouth* (final) 3.15 p.m. (40,500); total run, 96,830 papers, completed by 4 p.m. The three staffs worked in complete harmony and the arrangements were "as perfect as it was possible to make them". A pattern had been laid down which would be followed until Southampton and Weymouth offices were able to operate once more as independent units.

For one terrible moment in the summer of 1942, it seemed that all these elaborate arrangements had been in vain. A large bomb fell in the Upper Central Gardens at Bournemouth, about 200 yards from the *Echo* office. Happily, it fell on soft ground; had it fallen in the Square, enormous damage would have been done and the Company's one surviving plant might have been put out of action. In fact, there was only slight damage from shell splinters.

This narrow escape gave greater-than-ever urgency to the plans for building temporary works at Southampton on a site which had been secured in Janson Road, Shirley. The scheme was turned down by the Ministry of Works on the (misunderstood) grounds that the firm wanted reserve premises. But as a result of negotiations at all levels – national, regional and local – permission was eventually given for the erection of temporary premises on the original site in Above Bar and Portland Street. These were to include editorial offices, a Creed room and a composing room, adjoining the old press room, foundry and publishing department, which had survived the blitz.

A year later – in April, 1943 – the Bournemouth office was in even greater peril. During a daylight raid on the seaside resort, nearly every building in the Square and Christchurch Road was more or less damaged, and a Methodist Church almost opposite the *Echo* office was destroyed. The office itself, however, escaped with only a few broken windows.

In spite of the war, 1943 turned out to be one of the most successful years in the history of the Company. The annual report described the trading results as "again very satisfactory", and went on to inform the shareholders that "certain reconstruction work carried out during the year enabled production to be resumed at Southampton in May". This work was essentially of a temporary nature, and the cost was met out of current profits.

Important changes in the board and management took place during this year. In January 1943, Mr. E. J. Levi retired from the post of London Manager, after forty-three years, and was succeeded by Mr. W. J. Devoto. Mr. Levi, who was congratulated on "brilliant results", observed in his last report to the board that real progress in the history of the Company dated from the beginning of Mr. Gleave's period of office as General Manager. He also paid tribute to those who had served under him in the Fleet Street office, mentioning especially Messrs. L. G. Udall, Douglas Gleave, and Andrew Burnett, all of whom were to reach managerial status. The London blitz, he recalled, brought many difficulties, but the London office never "missed the boat" – or, rather, the train. On many occasions the parcel for Southampton had to be taken to Surbiton, Clapham or Balham when Waterloo was out of action. More than once incendiary bombs fell on the office, but Matthews, the caretaker (Military Medal and Bar), always had the situation well under control.

In July that year Sir Russell Bencraft relinquished the office of Chairman, owing to ill health, and was succeeded by Mr. W. A. Gleave. Sir Russell, who had been Chairman for eleven years and a director since 1904, remained on the board, and it was hoped that the Company would "continue to have the benefit of his long experience and valuable advice", but he died on Christmas Day.

In 1934, when Sir Russell completed thirty years as a director, he had commemorated the occasion by giving two monster parties, one for the *Southern Echo* and London office staffs, and one for the staffs of the *Bournemouth* and *Dorset Echos*. Among the important positions he held in the commercial life of Southampton was that of Chairman of Edwin Jones & Company Limited, and at the *Southampton Echo* party he caused much amusement by relating the following story:

"I was the doctor of the firm for many years, and when I retired they offered me a job in the building. It was a pretty good job, too. The first day I went on the job a lady, who had been a patient of mine, went up to one of the shop-walkers and inquired: 'What is Dr. Bencraft doing here?' The shop-walker replied: 'He has given up his profession, and he is working here now.' The lady's rejoinder was: 'Poor man. Drink, I suppose?'"

This was typical of Sir Russell's sense of humour. (He had also been physician to the Ordnance Survey, and used to tell how employees of that famous Government map-making department sometimes obtained admission to the County Cricket Ground by displaying prescriptions written in the indecipherable handwriting of Dr. Bencraft!)

Sir Russell was a man of wide interests, and cricket was perhaps his ruling passion. It was Sir Edwin Perkins who wrote of how much he was appreciated by his colleagues on the board, referring especially to his personal attention to the business of Southern Newspapers Limited (hardly a day passed without a head office visit from him) and to his "constant care for the welfare and happiness of the staff".

Looking through the records for 1944, we find that at Southampton the Company was employing two women Linotype operators who had learnt their job quickly and were good at it. (In the previous November the Chairman and General Manager – Mr. Gleave and Captain Jones – had visited London and placed orders for machinery.) In May, 1944, Messrs. R. Hoe and Company submitted final specifications for the new presses at Southampton. But though it was possible to plan ahead so far as equipment was concerned, there was much uncertainty about rebuilding. Locally there was a spirit of indecision, because nobody really knew what were the full

Above: Customers waiting for the first edition of the *Southern Echo* outside the temporary war-time office in Portland Street, Southampton.

Below: Directors and executives look on as Sir Robert Perkins, Chairman of Southern Newspapers Limited, cuts the first sod on the site of the new office.

Above: Bulldozing rubble left by the blitz to prepare the way for the new head office.

Below: Excavations for the office, facing Portland Street.

Above: Alderman Mrs. V. F. King, J.P., Mayor of Southampton, unveiling the foundation stone of the new office on December 29, 1953.

Below: Admiral of the Fleet Earl Mountbatten of Burma starts the presses after opening the Company's rebuilt headquarters.

Watching plates being machined and cooled after casting in the foundry of the new *Echo* building on opening day. *Left to right:* The Duke of Wellington (Lord Lieutenant of Hampshire), Mr. Ewen Montague, Q.C. (Recorder of Southampton), Alderman R. C. Chambers, J.P. (Director), Lady Patricia Perkins, Sir Robert Perkins (Chairman, Southern Newspapers Limited), the Countess Mountbatten of Burma, Earl Mountbatten of Burma, Alderman Mrs. M. O'Leary (Sheriff of Southampton).

implications of the Government's rebuilding plans. The Corporation was uncertain about how those plans were going to be put into effect, and already in 1944 acute differences of opinion had arisen between those who wanted the Council to buy up all sites in the central area, using compulsory powers if necessary, and those who thought that the principles of private ownership should not be disturbed.

It was indeed a time when the thoughts of many were turning to what might happen after the war. Among them was Mr. P. H. Thompson, Dorset Manager, who reported: "The *Dorset Daily Echo*, still being printed at Bournemouth, is going from strength to strength, despite severe production difficulties. Records have repeatedly been broken in all departments. The future promises progress on an extremely interesting scale, but a great deal will depend on how soon the *Dorset Echo* can be printed in its home town again after the end of hostilities."

First, hostilities had to be brought to an end. In 1944 there was still some tough fighting to get through, and among those involved in it were 150 employees of the Company, about a third of the total. It was the year of the Second Front, and as D-Day approached, Southampton "knew in its bones that a climax was at hand, despite the veil of secrecy that shrouded the coming operations", writes Knowles in his war history:

". . . without trumpets, the vast concourse of assault ships drew slowly away from Southampton Docks and, like a moving mosaic – 'the ships were so close together', writes an eyewitness, 'that it looked for all the world as though one could walk all the way to the Isle of Wight without wetting one's feet' – sailed without let or hindrance down Southampton Water to take up its place at the appointed rendezvous as the core of the invasion fleet. Thereafter, with every street full of excited whispers, the people of Southampton, intuitively aware of the greatness of the hour, but still in ignorance as to the true facts, suffered an agony of suspense. That same night it was heightened when, silhouetted against a sky of dull pearl, watchers saw what, in the words of one observer, looked like

I

'strings of sharks'. In reality they were Dakota-towed gliders heading for the Channel on the first stage of the most desperate military venture of all time. Even the staff of 'Area C' headquarters . . . were in no better plight than the public, and spent the hours of night watching and waiting for the news on which the world's destiny hung."

It was the greatest story of the war, but the *Echo* – in common with the rest of the British Press – could give no hint of what was going on.[1]

Those with a taste for statistics may be interested to know that during the seventeen weeks following D-Day the military tonnage handled by Southampton Docks was equivalent to the total imports and exports dealt with in the last complete peacetime year, 1938. Thousands of vessels entered and left the docks, millions of tons of freight passed over the quays, and three and a half million British, Commonwealth and American troops left Southampton during the twelve months that elapsed between D-Day and victory in Europe.

As the end of hostilities in Western Europe approached, the *Echo* announced that Nazism was dead – only the nerves in its loathsome tentacles still reacted. The task of those who had slain it was to "make certain it had not spawned in secret places". Then, on May 8, the paper announced the end of the war in Europe: "So, at last, we have come to the end of the road. It has been a long and weary way. Many gallant spirits are not with us to share in the joy of the goal achieved and the victory won. Our first thoughts today are with those who have given their lives that we may live, and with those who have been bereaved by the dreadful ravages of war. . . ."

The same note was struck by John Arlott in the commemor-

[1] The news broke on Tuesday, June 6, 1944. In a leading article entitled "The Great Crusade", the *Echo* said: "Good luck! From the depths of our hearts we repeat the fond wish; from the depths of our hearts we pray for those who have embarked upon the great adventure. . . . This is, at once, a splendid and a solemn day. The news that came so quickly after dawn loses none of its high drama by reason of the fact that it has been so long awaited. It was received quietly, calmly, almost with a sense of relief."

ative poem which the *Southern Echo* published in its V.E.-Day issue:

> *From wooden crosses in the sand*
> *The sad white discs of metal hang*
> *And quiet minds call back each night*
> *The sleeping men who lately sang.* . . .
>
> *A lance of fickle April sun*
> *Has flashed across the sullen skies*
> *To quicken winter seeds of life,*
> *And dead men live in children's eyes*

No one had looked forward to reconstruction after hostilities were over with greater intensity than Mr. Gleave, the Chairman, but failing health denied him that satisfaction. He died at the age of seventy-three on March 20, 1945, less than two months before V.E.-Day, having been associated with the Company for over half a century. His passing, coming as it did at the close of the war, seemed to mark the end of an epoch. During World War I he had devoted his scanty leisure to ambulance work in the Docks, for which he received the British Red Cross Medal, and to voluntary social work among Allied troops passing through the port, in recognition of which he was made an Officer of Public Instruction by the French Republic and was awarded the Golden Palms of the Order of the Crown of Belgium. During the last war he piloted the Company through the most difficult and treacherous shoals and currents it had ever encountered, and died just as it was about to enter the safe harbour of peace and victory. One of the earliest members of the Institute of Journalists (of which he was a Fellow) and recipient of one of the rare awards of the Company of Newspaper Makers, this distinguished pressman had celebrated his journalistic jubilee in 1936 at a united staff gathering, when more than 350 employees of the Company were present.

Appropriately enough, the vacancy on the board was filled by Mr. Gleave's old friend and colleague, Captain Jones, who had succeeded him as General Manager and Editor-in-chief. The new Chairman was Mr. W. R. D. (later Sir Robert) Perkins, Member of Parliament for Stroud, who returned to the board after temporary absence while a Junior Minister in the Coalition Government. Other directors at this time were Mr. H. Parsons, head of a well-known marine engineering company, and Colonel G. F. Perkins, C.B.E., D.S.O. Mr. R. I. Palmer had been appointed Secretary. The Company's consulting accountants were Messrs. Burnett, Swayne and Stothert, who had been associated with the firm during most of its history, and the auditors were Messrs. Woolley and Waldron.

CHAPTER 14

Reconstruction

THE FIRST TEN years of the post-war period were over-shadowed by reconstruction problems, and the Company owes much to the two men who, successively, held the office of General Manager during these difficult years – Captain Jones and Mr. C. F. Carr. For, on top of their normal duties, they had the task of carrying out the building programme which the board had drawn up even before hostilities had ended. This not only entailed regular conferences with architects and contractors, but prolonged – and often extremely frustrating – negotiations with planning authorities and Government departments.

A start was made at the end of 1945, when preliminary plans for a new Weymouth office were prepared and application was made for a licence to put up a building which at that time was estimated to cost £26,000.

The outlook in Southampton was bleak. Inability of the Corporation to agree on a central reconstruction plan meant that for at least five years businesses in the heart of the town would have to carry on their activities in temporary premises and with improvised equipment. So far as the Company was concerned, this proved to be an over-optimistic forecast, as it was not until 1952 that the first part of the new headquarters was completed.

The Company's most pressing need at Southampton was for photographic and block-making facilities (all work of this kind being done in Bournemouth at that time), and when a scheme was drawn up for new temporary offices on the Above Bar site, these facilities were provided on the roof of the paper store behind the garage. In the February of 1946 plans for the temporary Southampton premises were approved and the necessary building licences issued. At this time the authorities gave the Company the "Go ahead" at Weymouth.

In Southampton the situation became more complicated when the Corporation announced that it had applied to the Ministry of Town and Country Planning for an order declaring that the whole of the centre of the town should be subjected to compulsory purchase for the purpose of dealing with war damage. Evidently Southern Newspapers would have a fight on their hands. For it had all along been the Company's contention that their freehold did not in any way obstruct the redevelopment of the blitzed area and should not be disturbed. Counsel's advice was taken, and on July 18, 1946, the Company was one of 200 freeholders in central Southampton who lodged objections with the Ministry.

In the autumn of that year a town-planning inquiry – the first of several at which the Company gave evidence – was held, but nothing was decided then.

It was hoped that the return of peace would bring an early end of the newsprint shortage, but during these post-war years rationing of this all-important commodity continued. Papers remained small, yet the demand for advertising space rapidly grew with the resumption of normal trading activities. Much business had to be turned away – during one four-week period in 1946 over 200 columns were sacrificed – and at the same time the Company had to refuse the repeated requests of newsagents for more papers. "We are disappointing more and more people", sadly reported the Advertisement Manager-in-chief, Mr. Raymond Baker.

The first relaxation in the newsprint situation occurred at the end of the summer of 1946, making it possible for the *Football Echos* at Southampton, Bournemouth and Weymouth to resume publication, amid scenes of enthusiasm. The increase in supplies enabled the Company to expand the *Southern* and *Bournemouth Echos* from eight to twelve pages four times a week and to allow the circulations of these papers to reach ceilings of 60,000 and 40,000 respectively.

During its 100 years' history, the Company has received many tributes, but none, perhaps, has given greater pleasure and encouragement to all concerned than the following passage which occurred in an article on European unity which Sir (then Mr.) Winston Churchill contributed to the *Daily Telegraph* of December 31, 1946:

"On my return from Zürich I read in an English newspaper, the *Southern Daily Echo*, the following commentary on what I had said: 'Geographers point out that the continent of Europe is really the peninsula of the Asiatic land mass. The real demarcation between Europe and Asia is no chain of mountains, no natural frontier, but a system of beliefs and ideas which we call Western Civilisation. In the rich pattern of this culture there are many strands: the Hebrew belief in God; the Christian message of compassion and redemption; the Greek love of truth, beauty and goodness; the Roman genius for law. Europe is a spiritual conception, but if men cease to hold that conception in their minds, cease to feel its worth in their hearts, it will die.'

"The sentiments are so beautiful and their expression so fine an example of English prose, that I venture to quote them with due acknowledgments, and I trust they may resound far and wide and waken their response in every generous heart. Well may it be said, 'Let Europe arise'."

A few months later, at the Albert Hall rally held to launch the United Europe Movement, Mr. Churchill again quoted this *Echo* leading article in a speech which was broadcast by the B.B.C. and reported in newspapers throughout the world:

"At school we learned from the maps hung on the walls, and the advice of our teachers that there is a continent called Europe. I remember quite well being taught this as a child, and, after living a long time, I still believe it is true. However, professional geographers now tell us that the continent of Europe is really only the peninsula of the Asiatic land mass. I must tell you in all faith that I feel this would be an arid and uninspiring conclusion, and for myself I distinctly prefer what I was taught when I was a boy.

"It has been finely said by a young English writer, Mr. Sewell,[1] that the real demarcation between Europe and Asia is no chain of mountains, no natural frontier, but a system of beliefs and ideas which we call Western Civilisation. 'In the rich pattern of this culture', says Mr. Sewell, 'there are many strands: the Hebrew belief in God; the Christian message of compassion and redemption; the Greek love of truth, beauty and goodness; the Roman genius for law. Europe is a spiritual conception. But if men cease to hold that conception in their minds, cease to feel its worth in their hearts, it will die.'

"These are not my words, but they are my faith; and we are here to proclaim our resolve that the spiritual conception of Europe shall not die. We declare, on the contrary, that it shall live and shine, and cast a redeeming illumination upon a world of confusion and woe. . . ."

1947 was a year of difficulties. The fuel crisis, which resulted in the temporary closing down of many periodicals, brought fresh restrictions on newsprint for the Press generally. The circulation of the Company's papers had to be cut and their size reduced; the bottleneck in advertising grew worse than ever. The Marshall Plan brought a glimmer of hope, however. With the prospect of dollar aid on a vast scale, it was announced by the Government that over £5 million would be set aside for the purchase of newsprint.

Staffing problems were exacerbated by the chronic housing shortage, and in the summer of 1947 the board decided

---

[1] Gordon Sewell, the Company's chief leader-writer. In 1958 he was the recipient of one of the British Atlantic Committee's Journalism Awards for a series of articles on N.A.T.O. which appeared in the *Southern Echo*.

to buy several properties and convert them into flats for employees.

That November Mr. W. A. Park retired after forty-seven years as Editor of the *Bournemouth Echo*. He was succeeded by Mr. Rodney Andrew, who was later to become Editor of the *Southern Echo* and Deputy General Manager of the Company. Mr. Andrew had joined the reporting staff of the *Southern Echo* in 1929. During the war he was commissioned in the Royal Artillery and, after being invalided out of the Army, he joined the Press Gallery, first as a representative of *The Times* and then as a Parliamentary sketch-writer for the *Daily Telegraph*. Before returning to Southern Newspapers Limited as Editor of the *Bournemouth Echo*, he widened his experience as Editor of the *Jersey Morning News*, which he revived after the war.

In spite of the difficulties to which we have referred, the directors in their annual report for 1947 were able to congratulate the shareholders on a substantial increase in turnover, due principally to relaxation in the restrictions on the use of newsprint. They were also "pleased to report that the erection of modern offices and works at Weymouth has been commenced".

In 1948, during one of the many financial crises which punctuated the economic history of this country in the years following the end of the war, the Government withdrew the licence for rebuilding the Weymouth office. Since a start had been made at considerable cost, the Company was naturally alarmed. Fortunately, however, an official investigation into the progress already made resulted in the licence being restored.

June saw the retirement of Captain A. E. Jones and the appointment of Mr. C. F. Carr as General Manager and Editor-in-chief in his place. Captain Jones, who had completed half a century in the employment of the Company, was elected a member of the board shortly afterwards. When, on August 19, 1948, the *Southern Echo* celebrated its diamond jubilee, the recollections of Captain Jones brought back for those attending a celebration dinner the early days of the paper. (Viscount Portal was the guest of honour on that occasion.)

Another anniversary that year was the golden jubilee of the *Football Echo* at Southampton. Writing in the fiftieth birthday number, Mr. George White – who had succeeded Captain Jones as Sports Editor – recalled how the publication of the paper each Saturday night was announced by a rush of yelling newsboys down the narrow Spa Road into the town's main thoroughfare. He continued:

"On the dreariest nights the street was in an instant transformed – in colour and sporting enthusiasm. It was one of the features of pre-war Southampton Saturday night life. There were always big crowds awaiting the 'Yellow 'Un', especially in front of the gaily-lit Palace Theatre – which rubbed shoulders with the home of the *Echo* – with people either coming from or going into that landmark of southern variety, or massing before the well-stocked shop-windows, each with bright appeal. The tram-drivers had to clank their foot-bells insistently – almost pounding a way through the crowds. Above Bar, on Saturday night, was a place of animation, surging life, the happy point where Southampton's townsfolk threw off the cares of a week's toil – and had fun. The *Football Echo* was woven into that skein of things.

"Only twice has the paper's history been interrupted: when the lights went out, one by one, over Europe in World War I in 1914, and again in World War II in 1939. Steadily throughout the last fifty years, the *Football Echo* has built up a following of readers who have given the paper a place in their life – in town and country, in the big centres of population in the county, in the villages and hamlets, and beyond the borders of Hampshire.

"Its pledge to 'encourage and foster southern sport' has been kept steadily in the forefront of the policy of the paper by successive editors, and there have been only three during the fifty years – the late Mr. W. A. Gleave, J.P., from 1898 to 1900; Captain A. E. Jones, M.C., from 1900 to 1920; and the present editor, Mr. G. F. White,[1] from January 31, 1920, to date. . . ."

As a result of managerial reorganisation following the retirement of Captain Jones and the promotion of Mr. Carr to the position of chief executive of the company, Mr. R. R. Gleave – who since the early part of the war had been Assistant Editor of the *Southern Echo* – was appointed Deputy General Manager of the Company and Editor at Southampton. His place as Assistant Editor and Assistant Manager was taken by Mr. Geoffrey O'Connor, who for the past ten years or more had been chief reporter of the *Southern Echo*. (Mr. O'Connor had served on all three of the Company's evening papers, and had been associated with Mr. Carr in the pioneering days of the *Dorset Echo*.)

Southern Newspapers Limited was one of the newspaper publishing firms invited to submit evidence to the Royal Commission on the Press which was sitting at about this time. One of the questions it was asked to answer concerned the functions and authority of the principal officers of its publications. In reply, the Company stated that for the past forty or fifty years the policy of its papers had been independent in character. The only directive given by the board with regard to the presentation of news was that it should be absolutely fair. It was the responsibility of the Editor-in-chief to maintain this policy, and any instructions he might convey to the editors of the three papers from time to time were directed to this end. No directives were given to the respective editors indicating in any way that the news should be presented from any particular angle.

Here, perhaps, is the appropriate place to recall another of the Company's rare "policy statements". In a brochure published

[1] Mr. White retired in 1954, and was succeeded as Sports Editor and Editor of the *Football Echo* by Mr. A. E. Rawlings, former Hampshire tennis champion, who joined the reporting staff in 1928. Mr. White's elder brother – Mr. A. E. (Tiger) White, the cashier at Southampton – retired in 1948, being at that time the oldest serving employee of the Company. He joined the *Echo* in 1888, three months after the paper was started.

in connection with the opening of the new office at Southampton, the writer had this to say: "The first function of a
newspaper is to give the news – adequately, reliably, brightly
and impartially. This we strive to do with all the aids that can
be provided by the latest techniques of news-gathering and
newspaper production, and with an editorial staff which under-
stands the needs, the problems and the psychology of the
region. In . . . the mid-Wessex counties the public looks for
evening newspapers which, though up-to-date in presentation
and appearance, are not in thrall to Fleet Street and Shoe Lane
– newspapers which reflect the life and interests of the local
community without neglecting the wider issues of the nation
and world. And that is what we aim to give our readers. . . .

"When the *Southern Echo* was founded by Passmore Edwards, the Victorian philanthropist, it had a party political
policy, although from the first its news columns have always
been impartial. For many years, however, it has followed a
strictly independent line in its editorials, and this it will continue to do. But, while jealously guarding its independence,
the *Echo* fights for the causes and ideals in which it believes. It
was in the course of a comment on this editorial policy that the
Fortnightly Review some years ago described the *Echo* as 'an
original and intelligent newspaper'. . . ."

★   ★   ★

There followed a year of achievement. In 1949 a Newport
office was opened, thus enabling the *Southern Echo* to publish
an Isle of Wight edition with late news printed in. A greater
plentifulness of newsprint made possible larger papers and increased circulation. In April Messrs. Ellis, Clarke and Gallan-
naugh of London were appointed architects for the new head
office building, and at the first meeting between the architects
and Company executives the special difficulties which would
have to be faced were gone into and a phasing scheme worked
out which would enable the *Southern Echo* to be published
without interruption while building operations were in progress.

In the July the new office at Weymouth was opened by Sir David Ross, Chairman of the Royal Commission on the Press. Printing at Weymouth had been resumed some weeks previously, on June 13. After seven years and two months, the *Dorset Echo* was back in its home town, with a better news service and better equipment than before the war. The change-over took place during a week-end, the machines being brought by road from Bournemouth and installed ready for the Monday's printing.

The old bogy of compulsory purchase returned in the autumn, when the Company was informed of the Southampton Corporation's intention to acquire its freehold in Above Bar and Portland Street. The board was as determined as ever to fight the local authority over this issue, and Mr. Carr and Captain Jones were sent to Reading to explain to the Regional Controller, Major-General Coxwell Rogers, that if the Council persisted in its policy of compulsorily purchasing the site, the Company would not rebuild on it.

What happened during these weeks is best told in the words of Sir (then Mr.) Robert Perkins, the Chairman. At the 1949 annual meeting he informed the shareholders:

"Towards the end of last year it looked as if, at long last, we were going ahead. To understand what has happened recently it is necessary that you should realise that the only obstacle to progress up till that time was the uncertainty as to the Southampton Borough Council's attitude to compulsory purchase. Like the other freeholders in the block in which our land is situated, we were – and still are – opposed to compulsory purchase. Southampton Borough Council, it is true, decided in November last year to schedule the area concerned for compulsory purchase, but, up to the present, this decision had not been implemented.

"The town planning officials then produced a development plan for the area. This imposed heavy restrictions upon us in regard to the use of the considerable area of land we own facing on to Above Bar. Conformity with the Town Plan further placed upon us the necessity of acquiring certain pieces of land from adjacent freeholders, although we already had ample land for our planning needs.

"Although we opposed compulsory purchase, we accepted the Town Plan for the area, with all the disadvantages it meant for us. This was our voluntary contribution to the building of the New Southampton.

"We were advised by experts we consulted that acceptance of the Block Development Scheme and arrangements among all the freeholders concerned to resolve, by mutual agreement, our individual planning difficulties would probably stave off compulsory purchase. This view was in fact reflected by Borough Council officials, with whom we have been in continual consultation and discussion for many months. We were definitely encouraged to go ahead on these lines. We did so.

"Last April we appointed one of the finest firms of newspaper-building architects in the country. . . . Then followed months of intensive planning – at all stages, mark you, in full consultation with the Borough officials concerned. It is an interesting fact, too, that we had agreed to go much further than the planning of our own building. At the specific request of the local authority, we instructed our architects to prepare suggested elevations for the entire block. At the definite request of the local authority we accepted the responsibility of setting the standard of design for the block. . . .

"Our preliminary plans were, in due course, placed before the relevant committee. We were told that they had received, even at that stage, a substantial degree of approval. In mid-August, our own plans, together with a full statement of our need for rebuilding, were sent by our architects to the regional offices at Reading of the Ministry of Town and Country Planning, the Board of Trade and the Ministry of Works.

"Then, about a fortnight later, came a sudden approach, indicating that the issue of compulsory purchase had again arisen. We at once pressed for a clarification of the position. As a result, the Reconstruction Sub-committee of the

Southampton Borough Council have intimated that they are unable to recommend the Council to reverse their decision to make a Compulsory Purchase Order for the block, but indicating that they will meet representatives of Southern Newspapers Limited to discuss the question of development on the basis of acquisition of the site by the Corporation and the granting of a lease to this Company. . . .

"Our policy in this matter is quite clear: if compulsory purchase is, in fact, applied by Southampton Borough Council to the area in which our land is situated, we do not intend to rebuild our works there. . . ."

This was no empty threat. Sites were investigated at Totton and Eastleigh, but these places did not qualify as war-damaged towns for the allocation of building materials.

Fortunately, it did not become necessary to look elsewhere, for on October 19, 1950, Southampton Council reversed its policy concerning the compulsory purchase of property in Above Bar between Spa Road and Portland Street.

It was at last possible to make real progress with the rebuilding scheme. In January, 1951, town-planning consent to the first phase was received; in March contracts were signed with the architects and the contractors, Messrs. W. E. Chivers and Sons, of Devizes, builders of Harwell and Aldermaston atomic stations.

As soon as the actual building of phase 1 was started, planning application for further building licences was made. It was stated at this time that complications arising out of the country's defence programme would result in a clamping down on licences in 1952.

The difficulties being experienced by the *Southern Echo* were explained by Mr. Carr in a letter to the Regional Controller of the Board of Trade at Reading:

"It will be realised that we are rebuilding a large newspaper works on a site on which we have been producing the *Southern Daily Echo* in temporary accommodation since 1943. We have to maintain the production of the *Echo* in these temporary buildings on the rebuilding site throughout the whole period of our scheme. The *Southern Echo*, as it has been emphasised before, is not only the sole local evening newspaper, but it services a tremendously wide area, which includes the Isle of Wight, the New Forest, a large portion of eastern Hampshire, and the greater part of southern, northern and western Hampshire, as well as a considerable portion of Wiltshire.

"As soon as we received our licence, the first thing we had to do was to knock down the eastern walls of our existing press room and excavate part of its flooring. This deprived us of a good third of our temporary press room accommodation. It also deprived us of several large workshops and storage space. The press room space remaining has had to be walled in again with temporary walls. The electrical supply, not only to the press room, but to the whole of our existing works, now comes from a temporary cable. In addition, the present work has necessitated the removal of certain other facilities and the installation of temporary tanks, furnaces, etc. Generally speaking, our works staff, who have been working under tremendously difficult conditions ever since 1943, are now worse off than at any time before. . . ."

The purpose of this letter was to convince the Board of Trade that nothing should be allowed to hold up the Company's rebuilding scheme, and in this it appears to have been successful. During 1952 the necessary licences were issued to enable the orderly phasing of the work to continue, although at one time it looked as though everything would come to a standstill as a result of a misunderstanding over 20 tons of steel rods. Correspondence between the Chairman and the President of the Board of Trade helped to put matters right. But though the *Echo* scheme enjoyed a high priority, there were times when, to quote the architects, the materials supply position was "hopelessly chaotic" and delays in deliveries slowed down the tempo of the work. During all this time the costs of machinery and equipment were soaring.

★   ★   ★

Meanwhile, the Company had been losing, through death,

City of Southampton

To Southern Newspapers Limited

Greetings

At a meeting of the Southampton City Council held on the twentieth day of May One thousand nine hundred and sixty-four it was

Resolved that this Council extend to Southern Newspapers Limited their sincere congratulations on the celebration of their Centenary and record that the Council have always enjoyed the fullest co-operation with the local Press. They feel assured that the happy association and understanding will continue

These presents recite this Resolution as a record of appreciation of the services of Southern Newspapers Limited to the City of Southampton

Given under the Corporate Seal of the Mayor, Aldermen and Citizens of the City and County of the City of Southampton this twentieth day of May One thousand nine hundred and sixty-four

Mayor

Town Clerk

The resolution congratulating Southern Newspapers Limited on their centenary, passed by Southampton City Council.

Behind these Wessex Saints in the great west window of St. Mary's, Southampton's Mother Church, is portrayed the new headquarters of Southern
Newspapers Limited.

The floodlit colonnade of the *Echo* building on opening day made a striking
contribution to the night scene in Southampton's Above Bar.

A horse and trap used to distribute the *Southern Echo* in the early days of the newspaper.

One of the Company's first motor delivery vans (1914).

some of its stalwarts: Mr. E. J. Levi, former London Manager (July, 1950), Mr. Harry Parsons, Director (February, 1951) and Mr. F. E. Stevens, former Editor of the *Hampshire Advertiser*, which had ceased publication in 1940. Mr. Stevens – "Freddie" to all who knew him – had an encyclopaedic knowledge of Hampshire past and present, and was an authority on the New Forest, the subject of one of his many books.

Here it should be mentioned that on October 6, 1950, the *Bournemouth Echo* celebrated its golden jubilee and that in October, 1952, a branch office was opened at Andover and a manager-reporter appointed.

On December 1, 1952, the *Southern Echo* moved into part one of its new home – the section facing Portland Street – following a hectic but well-planned twenty-four-hour change-over from the old temporary buildings.

This first section temporarily housed the entire composing production plant, as well as the publishing department and all the editorial offices. The rest of the site was now ready to be cleared for the next section of the building, which would include part of the new press room.

In 1952 it looked as though the industry's newsprint diffi-culties were over at last. In the August it was announced that freedom of consumption had been restored, subject only to limitation on the number of pages. (The *Southern* and *Bourne-mouth Echos* could now go up to twenty pages a day, although in fact they did not at this time exceed sixteen pages.) But after only four months of this new freedom the Government announced that it would have to impose limitations on news-print imports from dollar sources during the first half of 1953.

The 1953 annual report stated that "at the close of the financial year your directors were negotiating for a controlling interest in the Bournemouth Times Limited".

Behind this bald statement lay a dramatic story. The *Bournemouth Times* had been offered to Southern Newspapers Limited on several occasions, and although the Company had declined, there was an informal understanding with Mr.

K

James Putnam, the principal proprietor of the *Bournemouth Times*, that if ever he decided to sell the property he would inform Sir Robert Perkins before completing any deal.

One day in the summer of 1953 he phoned the Chairman to say that he was selling to Mr. Roy Thomson, the famous Canadian newspaper proprietor, the very next day. The Chairman immediately made arrangements for an emergency board meeting, which assembled at Southampton the following morning. Another phone conversation was held with Mr. Putnam, who said: "I'd rather sell to Southern Newspapers, but you'll have to hurry, because the deal with Thomson is due to be concluded at 2.30 this afternoon."

Convinced that Mr. Thomson had plans to use the plant of the *Times* for the production of an evening paper in competition with the *Bournemouth Echo*, the board decided to buy a controlling interest, and empowered Captain Jones and Mr. R. I. Palmer, the Secretary, to negotiate the purchase as soon as possible. This meant a dash by car to Bournemouth, and as the two men entered the *Bournemouth Times* building the clock was striking half-past two! They were met at the entrance hall by James Putnam, who greeted them with the words: "I'm so glad you've arrived in time. Thomson's accountants are in there" – indicating a closed door – "waiting to sign."

Within half an hour Mr. Putnam and the representatives of Southern Newspapers had come to terms. The following day another special board meeting was held at Southampton, where an agreement was drafted on the spot by the Company Secretary. Thus Southern Newspapers Limited acquired the whole of the issued capital of the Bournemouth Times Limited, and of Hardy Press Limited, a subsidiary which handled contract printing work for the *Times*.

This has proved to be one of the most important investments made by the Company during its history. The purchase brought into the Southern Newspapers group three weeklies – the *Bournemouth Times*, the *Poole and Dorset Herald* and the *Swanage Times* – to which a fourth, the *Christchurch Herald*, was added in 1960. Even more important, from a financial point of view, it brought what was potentially (and is now in fact) one of the finest printing houses in the country. During the past ten years the *Bournemouth Times* plant has been almost entirely re-equipped and a German M.A.N. press for colour work – the first and only one in Britain – has been installed. In these works are printed some of the country's best-known periodicals. (In 1964 another printing firm – W. H. Hallett Limited, of Poole – was acquired to take over the *Bournemouth Times'* jobbing business.) In the same year, 1953, Mr. Douglas Gleave succeeded Mr. R. Fairbairn as Manager of the *Bournemouth Echo*.

★   ★   ★

In 1954 a scrip issue was made of one fully paid up £1 share for every two £1 shares held, thus increasing the issued capital of the Company to £484,160. This was one of several scrip issues which have been made over the years, and was typical of the way in which the Company's finances have been handled throughout its existence. It has always been the policy of the board to plough part of the profits back, and in this way the capital has grown during the past 100 years from some £12,000 in 1864 to £1,210,400 in this centenary year, without the Company going to the public on a single occasion, although some "rights" issues have been made to shareholders.

It was in fact a scrip issue of one share for two in February, 1964, which brought the capital to the latter figure. Indeed, it may be said that the Company's prosperity is based partly on the fact that the directors have always adopted a conservative policy in the distribution of profits, and have thus been able to build up reserves from which to finance development. At the same time they have kept the welfare of the staff in mind, setting aside at regular intervals increasing sums of money for the Benevolent and Pensions Fund. (The Company's pensions scheme is non-contributory, and is based on length of service and salary at the time of retirement.)

★   ★   ★

This year the board was strengthened by the appointment of

Mr. P. J. B. Perkins as an additional director. Staff changes included the retirement of the Sports Editors at Southampton and Bournemouth – Mr. George F. White (forty-four years' service) and Mr. P. H. Yeats, respectively; the retirement of Mr. W. H. Hill, Editor of the *Dorset Daily Echo* (thirty-two years' service), and Mr. W. J. Devoto, London Manager. Mr. Hill was succeeded by Mr. A. R. Adlam and Mr. Devoto by Mr. Leonard Udall.

On Monday, November 21, 1955, the hopes and strivings of many years found fulfilment when the handsome bronze doors of Southern Newspaper's new headquarters in Above Bar were officially opened by Admiral Earl Mountbatten of Burma, who was accompanied by the Countess ("Lady Louis", as she will always be remembered) and a representative gathering of eminent people drawn from public life all over the county.

To commemorate the occasion, the company presented Lady Mountbatten with an antique silver box, and in expressing her thanks she said she would value this gift all the more because the *Echo* was her favourite newspaper. "I remember reading the *Echo* when I was first able to read, and my old nanny spelling out certain words for me," she added.

"It has cost a lot of money",[1] Sir Robert Perkins told the shareholders at the annual general meeting that autumn, "but we have built the cost into solid assets which not only maintain their value over the years in service and production terms, but which may also produce some capital accretion."

On this historic occasion the *Southern Echo* looked back on sixty-seven years of continuous publication in the great port of Southampton. With the completion of the fine building which was now its permanent home, the newspaper began a fresh and exciting chapter in its history.

The new headquarters occupies a central position in South-ampton's main shopping street and extends along Spa Road and Portland Street to Portland Terrace – a neighbourhood rich

[1] The total cost of building and equipping the new head office was approximately £1 million.

in historical associations where, in Georgian times, princes and aristocrats came to "take the waters". It was not without significance that the *Echo* building, symbol of the New Southampton which had risen out of the debris left by the war, should stand on a site which was famous during the town's Spa period. For it has always been the policy of the Company to cherish tradition as well as to advocate progress. In its new building it does more than advocate progress, for this splendid modern unit for producing a daily newspaper incorporates in its design and equipment all that is most up to date in newspaper technology.

Here are huge presses capable of printing 180,000 copies of the *Echo* an hour . . . batteries of Linotype, Ludlow and Elrod casting machines, on which type for the paper is set up, housed in the cool, clean atmosphere of a cream-tiled composing room . . . teleprinter machines of the latest pattern which, through the day, spell out news which reaches the *Echo* from every part of the earth . . . the magical apparatus which receives and prints wire photos . . . quiet offices where the writing is done. And in every part of this great building there are well-chosen colour schemes to cheer the spirits, acoustic ceilings to cushion off the noise of machines and fluorescent lamps to give it daylight round the clock.

Architecturally, the Company's headquarters make an impressive and pleasing contribution to Southampton's reconstructed commercial centre. The façade in Above Bar has been given a contemporary treatment in brick and Portland stone, and the effect of its recessed colonnade (behind which are the editorial and executive offices and the board room of the Company), of its bronze doors and bronze-framed windows, and of its large external clock is one which combines most happily functional simplicity and traditional grace. We like to think that the esteem in which the Company is held, and the trust which its publications inspire, are suitably symbolised by the portrayal of this fine building in one of the new stained-glass windows in St. Mary's, Southampton's mother church.

"Naturally", ran a statement issued by the Company at this time, "we are proud of our new building, but we do not pretend that bricks and mortar, concrete, glass and steel make a newspaper. The *Echo*, we claim, has its own personality, distinct and unmistakeable, which has developed over long years. Certainly it continued to find expression when our previous head office was a heap of smouldering ruins. And although this time we have built in hope and trust for the future, we believe the spirit of the *Echo* will survive even the deep concrete foundations and the tall steel frames of its new home.

"The *Echo* has grown up with modern Southampton. Although there has been a port at this junction of three waterways since Roman times, it is only within the life-span of the *Echo* that Southampton has come right to the fore as the nation's greatest passenger port. Today it is that and something more. Reaping the benefits of post-war recovery and of the technological revolution of our time, the town which we serve has become the most important industrial centre in the South.

"This new prosperity is by no means confined to the borough boundaries of Southampton. It extends east, west and north into Hampshire and Wiltshire. Typifying this remarkable growth of the last decade is the vast oil refinery at Fawley, whose modernistic plant, like a Wellsian fantasy of the future, occupies a strip of Forest shore which only a few years ago was deserted parkland. As the region has grown in economic strength and population, the *Echo* has grown with it, stimulating the trend of industry and commerce as only a first-class advertising medium can. The *Echo* has indeed met the challenge of these exciting years, in spite of restricted plant and inadequate premises, in spite of newsprint rationing and all the other handicaps which a war-wounded newspaper without a proper home was bound to experience in a difficult period of transition.

"We believe that with the coming of nuclear energy for industry and the development of revolutionary manufacturing methods, no limit can be set to the prosperity of this part of England, and it is with enthusiasm that we look forward to playing our part, as a daily newspaper, in the thrilling tasks which lie ahead of Southampton and the South generally."

One way in which the Company has contributed to the economic growth of the region is by publishing, from each of its centres at Southampton, Bournemouth and Weymouth, an annual industrial survey. Beginning in 1953, this survey has steadily grown in comprehensiveness and authority over the years, and its publication is now an important and much-looked-forward-to event in the industrial community of the mid-South.

In his 1955 annual meeting address, the Chairman mentioned that the year had seen the introduction of a new competitor in British advertising. "The advent of commercial television," he said, "is obviously an important event capable of bringing about much economic and social change. No one can predict what its effect on Press advertising will be." (Our friendly rivals in the fields of advertising and news coverage, Southern Television Limited, opened their studios at Northam, Southampton, in 1958.)

Changes among the Company's financial officers were announced at this meeting. Owing to his retirement from public practice, Mr. H. A. H. Swayne, joint auditor with Mr. F. L. Woolley since 1949, did not wish to be reappointed, and his place was taken by Mr. J. P. Burnett, a senior partner of Messrs. Burnett, Swayne and Co. It was recalled that Mr. Burnett's father, the late Mr. E. G. Burnett, had been Secretary to the Company for thirty-four years until his death in 1941, and that Mr. John Burnett was himself Secretary from 1941 to 1945, although unable to serve actively because of his absence on war service in the Royal Navy. Mr. Swayne's grandfather and his father were successively Joint Auditors during the years 1864 to 1914.

In February, 1956, the death occurred of Mr. R. C. Chambers, J.P., who had joined the board five years previously. His great knowledge both of finance and of local conditions – he was Chairman of the famous Romsey brewing firm, Strong

& Company – were much appreciated by his fellow directors.

The vacancy thus arising on the board was filled by the appointment as a director of Mr. Sidney E. Whitehead, O.B.E., J.P., who was for many years General Manager of the old Southampton Gaslight and Coke Company and later Deputy Chairman of the Southern Gas Board.

Commenting on the opening of the new headquarters, Sir Robert Perkins had this to say at the annual meeting held in October, 1956:

"It was a great day for Southern Newspapers Limited, and it marked the culmination of ten years' hard work, first to overcome the obstacles which prevented an earlier start with the rebuilding of our blitzed works and then the actual planning, building and equipping of what many experts who have seen it tell us is one of the finest newspaper establishments in the kingdom.

"But the whole task of the final resettlement of our departments there has not yet been completed. There is still a considerable amount of work to be done, and it is now proceeding apace. The heaviest job of work yet to be finished is the building of the second part of the new press room and the installation of the third large rotary press, which was manufactured at the same time as the two new rotaries now in use, and which is now in store at Southampton awaiting erection as soon as the builders have finished their part of the rebuilding work.

"The old rotaries were taken down some months ago; one was sold and the other reconstructed and erected in the press room of the *Dorset Daily Echo* at Weymouth.

"You will thus see that we have made adequate provision, not only to meet our present needs, but for the future, in that there is room for the erection of the fourth press when this becomes necessary at some time in the future."

It was also reported that in order to carry out contracts for printing periodicals at the *Bournemouth Times* plant and to allow for future expansion of this type of business, it had been necessary to order a new rotary press and to undertake the construction of a new press room at the Branksome works.

CHAPTER 15

Years of Expansion

ANOTHER YEAR MARKED by important changes in the management of the Company was 1957. That summer Mr. C. F. Carr retired from the position of General Manager and Editor-in-chief. He had joined the Company at Weymouth in 1921 and soon afterwards became Assistant Manager and Assistant Editor at Southampton. As the Chairman remarked at the 1957 annual meeting, Mr. Carr had served Southern Newspapers well as its chief executive officer, having been responsible for bringing the rebuilding of the Southampton office to completion and having supervised the installation of its up-to-date machinery.

In Mr. Carr's place the board appointed Mr. R. R. Gleave, J.P., who had spent his working life in the service of the Company. He started as a junior reporter in 1920, became the *Southern Echo*'s specialist in shipping matters, and was appointed Assistant Manager and Assistant Editor in 1941. Six years later he succeeded Mr. Carr as Deputy General Manager of the Company and Editor of the *Southern Echo*. On being appointed chief executive of the Company, he had the satisfaction of following in the footsteps of his father, who had filled that office with such distinction during the years 1924-41.

Mr. Gleave's place as Deputy General Manager and Editor of the *Southern Echo* was filled by the transfer of Mr. Rodney Andrew, J.P., from Bournemouth, where he had most successfully edited the *Bournemouth Daily Echo* for the previous ten years. Mr. G. W. O'Connor was offered promotion, but, owing to the operation of the age limit, which would have prevented him from succeeding to the General Managership, he retained, at his own request, his present appointment as Assistant Manager and Assistant Editor of the *Southern Echo*. Mr. Douglas Sims was appointed editor at Bournemouth, where he had for several years been chief sub-editor.

In 1956-7, for the first time since the outbreak of World War II, international events had adversely affected the finances of the Company. "For many months on end", said the Chairman in his speech on October 22, 1957, "there was a heavy depression hanging over industry, in which the Government credit squeeze and hire-purchase restrictions, aimed at the control of inflation, adversely affected business. Then followed the Suez crisis, as well as the uncertainty over Cyprus. Interspersed with these other factors was petrol rationing and, later, industrial unrest.

"All these factors, quite beyond our control, very adversely affected our position in the first half of the financial year. . . . There was a sharp fall in national advertising, mainly due to the impact of commercial television, but with the arrival of autumn our expectations were being fulfilled. Then came the Middle East crisis to cloud the horizon, causing us heavy losses in advertising, as none was received from the petrol companies during the whole period of petrol rationing. New-car advertising virtually disappeared, and that of second-hand cars was severely curtailed. Transport difficulties adversely affected retail trade, and advertisers tended to cut space accordingly. It was certainly a winter of discontent, and ended with strikes in dockland and other local industries."

Fortunately, the position was largely retrieved by the special steps taken by the board. These included increasing the prices of the Company's publications and raising the advertising rates.

This was a time when the high cost of newsprint and other rising expenses was resulting in the closing down of many well-known provincial newspapers. "But," the Chairman was able to announce, "with our two blitzed offices rebuilt, we are now in a sound position to weather such storms as may arise."

At Southampton the task of rebuilding was virtually completed. During the year the second part of the press room had been rebuilt and the third rotary press installed. This additional press capacity enabled the *Southern Echo* to print specialised editions for the districts served by the paper and thus to increase its circulation.

During the same period the new process-engraving and photographic departments came into operation and the new publishing room was opened.

There now began what looked like being the most remarkable period of expansion in the history of the Company with the opening of a branch office at Hythe on Southampton Water in the spring of 1958. These premises enabled the *Echo* to improve considerably its news service in the New Forest area.

On July 1, 1958, the titles of the Company's newspapers were changed from "Daily" to "Evening": the three papers were now to be called the *Southern Evening Echo*, the *Evening Echo, Bournemouth*, and the *Dorset Evening Echo*. This emphasis on late news was supported by the growing number of editions which were being published. During this same period, the Press Association wire-photo service started at Southampton.

By now the Company had a circulation department active throughout its territory, with Mr. A. L. Cross as its Manager. The vigour shown by him and his staff – coupled with the policy of opening new branch offices and improving news coverage wherever possible – soon bore fruit in an accelerated growth of readership. As the centenary year dawned, the average daily audited circulation figures were: *Southern Evening Echo*, 97,780, *Evening Echo, Bournemouth*, 64,173, *Dorset Evening Echo*, 21,410.

The next branch office to be opened was at Alton (in the September of 1958), which enabled the *Southern Echo* to return to a district in which it was well-established before the war. A year later – on October 6, 1959 – the new Winchester office in Upper Brook Street was opened.

The *Echo* had occupied an office in the Cathedral city's High Street since 1921. When these premises began to prove inadequate, the firm looked for alternative accommodation in a neighbourhood which was being re-developed to provide Winchester with a new business centre, up-to-date, yet in keeping with the city's ancient background.

"Echo House" – as the office is called – epitomises in many ways the spirit of Winchester. Like the city, it is old, yet adapted to modern uses. Like Winchester, it has charm and dignity. Dating from the eighteenth century, it was at one time a hostelry, the Plough Inn. As Sir Robert Perkins told the civic authorities at a cocktail party held to celebrate the opening, the firm was grateful for the opportunity of saving a priceless old building occupying a Roman site.

This year's record also contained other evidence of healthy growth. In order to gain colour experience, the Company decided to publish its own annual calendar – the *Wonderful Wessex Calendar*. Besides proving a *succès d'estime*, the venture has been a profitable one. Some 12,500 copies are now being sold annually.

At Bournemouth the Company sold half the New Theatre Royal site adjoining the Richmond Hill works and offices and retained the remainder for expansion.

In the summer of 1959 a dark shadow suddenly fell across these bright prospects when the national printers' strike shut down all the Company's publications. The three *Evening Echos*, which never missed an edition throughout the air-raids, were now off the streets for the first time.

Thanks to the arbitration of Lord Birkett, the strike was settled, and publication was resumed on August 4. The editorial and commercial staffs had continued working during the six weeks' stoppage, but all the mechanical departments had been affected by the strike, which cost the Company many thousands of pounds lost in revenue.

Mr. Baker, the Advertisement Manager-in-chief, reported to the board that the revenue for July, 1959, was a mere £500 compared with some £30,000 during the same month in 1958. "We cannot yet begin to lick our wounds; we do not know how deep they are," he said. "The prolonged stoppage has not only lost us practically all the advertising which would have appeared since June 20, but, by continuing into the normally quiet period, it has made the task of resuming business much more difficult."

Our big advertisers used various expedients during the strike – television, notices in buses, loudspeaker vans, sky-writing, direct mail. But there was no substitute for the small ad., and when publication was resumed the back-log of "classifieds" was enormous.

Nevertheless, "business continued to expand and satisfactory results were shown, in spite of the printing dispute," stated the 1959 annual report.

The same report recorded the retirement from the board of Captain A. E. Jones, "in view of his advanced age", after an association with the Company totalling sixty-one years. (Captain Jones continued to serve on the board of the Bournemouth Times Limited.) Mr. S. E. Whitehead, O.B.E., J.P., also retired (on account of ill-health), and the two vacancies were filled by the appointment of Mr. R. R. Gleave and Mr. R. I. Palmer as Directors. It was recalled that Mr. Palmer's association with the Company dated from 1923; he was appointed Assistant Secretary in 1941 and Secretary in 1945.

In January, 1960, Mr. P. H. Thompson retired as Weymouth Manager after thirty years, and was succeeded by Mr. H. S. F. Kimber of the Southampton advertisement staff. When, just over a year later – in March, 1961 – the death occurred of Mr. H. R. E. Baker, Mr. Kimber was recalled from Weymouth to take his place as Advertisement Manager-in-chief, and Mr. Andrew Burnett was appointed Weymouth Manager.

At the annual meeting in the autumn of 1960, the directors were able to report that "detailed plans for the extension of the

Bournemouth premises by utilising land available from the Theatre Royal site are now completed, and work has commenced".

The shareholders were also informed: "The Company's present 'objects' were drawn up in 1864 and, in view of the possibility of the establishment of local commercial radio stations, the directors are of the opinion that the 'objects' of the Company should now be extended to enable it to participate in the dissemination of news by the modern means of radio or television broadcasting as well as by the circulation of newspapers."

This was agreed to, and as a consequence a company known as Voice of the South Limited was registered with a nominal capital. Later, other companies were registered for the purpose of safeguarding Southern Newspapers' interests in the Southampton, Bournemouth and Basingstoke areas, should commercial sound radio be permitted at any time in the future.

On May 28, 1961, the *Dorset Evening Echo* celebrated its fortieth anniversary. Its front page had been redesigned with a coloured seal and title, thus bringing it into line with the front pages of the Bournemouth and Southampton papers. At the same time, provision was made for stop press on the back page. The youngest of the group's evening papers was soon to be served by a new branch office at Bridport. (Two years later, in 1963, great pleasure was given throughout the group when the *Dorset Echo* won one of the annual awards for newspaper design; this justified the faith the Company had shown in its "Benjamin" by re-equipping the Dorset plant.)

Most important event for the Company in 1961 was the opening of part of the extension at Bournemouth. This was marked by a civic ceremony, when the Mayor of the town started the first of the two new presses on September 8, sixty-one years after one of his predecessors had started the paper's first press.

The extension, which cost half a million pounds, was not completed, however, until the following September. It turned out to be one of the trickiest jobs in the history of building in Bournemouth. The contractors – Messrs. W. E. Chivers and Sons Limited – had the formidable task of both organising the existing premises and erecting the new premises on adjoining land. Their greatest difficulty was caused by lack of space, and during nearly all the time the work was in progress they had no proper storage accommodation for their materials.

The extension was initially planned to meet the urgent and essential demands of a rapidly-growing newspaper business. But the final scheme included new accommodation for technical processes, social rooms for the staff, a basement paper store and a ground-floor vehicle area for the internal loading and unloading of delivery vans.

The building operations had to be carried out at the same time as the existing works, including the press room, were being reorganised. Two new presses were installed, and a new foundry to serve the press room was provided in the extension.

When the architects – Messrs. Weston, Burnett and Thorne, of Southampton – came to plan the extension, their immediate problem was to provide easy and efficient access for the delivery vans of a newspaper building bounded by two one-way streets. This was overcome by building an underground ramp to enable vans to be driven direct from Albert Road to Yelverton Road. (Those readers who are familiar with the traffic problems of down-town Bournemouth will appreciate what this means.)

One of the most interesting but least obvious aspects of the extension was the concrete basement running across the full width of the premises, which provides storage space for up to 300 tons of newsprint. For this it was necessary to build reinforced, waterproof concrete walls and floors, the walls being 18 inches thick. This "raft" formed the foundation for the structural steel framework of the building above the ground, on which rested the pre-cast concrete floors designed to carry the presses and other heavy machinery.

It was, of course, necessary to exercise extreme care when

excavating the ground to form this deep basement, in order to maintain adequate support for the walls of the existing *Echo* building on one side and the New Theatre Royal opposite, as well as the roadways on the two other sides.

With the installation of two new three-unit Hoe and Crabtree printing presses, it was now possible to produce forty-eight-page editions of the *Bournemouth Echo*.

Before the modernisation at Bournemouth was completed, the *Southern Echo* re-established itself in the growing north Hampshire town of Basingstoke. The paper had circulated there up till the war, and its return – warmly welcomed by local civic leaders – coincided with plans for town expansion to take a large overspill of population from London. A branch office in Cross Street was opened early in 1961. Two years later the Company opened negotiations, which proved to be of a prolonged nature, for the acquisition of much larger premises at 16 Church Street, Basingstoke, the Cross Street office having been quickly outgrown as a result of rapidly increasing sales of the paper. After extensive structural work has taken place, it is hoped that the new office will be opened late in the centenary year.

Here it is appropriate to record that in the latter part of 1961 the Dorchester office was modernised, and that in the spring of 1963 the *Southern Evening Echo* moved from its old Salisbury premises in The Canal into its new office, 2 Castle Street.

During 1962 the *Southern Echo* extended its circulation area to Warminster; and the company joined the Audit Bureau of Circulations and the Evening Newspapers Advertising Bureau. On January 1 Mr. Denys Treseder, who had entered the Company's service some years previously as Deputy Sports Editor at Southampton, was appointed Executive Assistant at head office. At this time an important technical event in the history of the Company was the publication of the first coloured advertisements in the *Southern* and *Bournemouth Echos*.

That March Southern Newspapers suffered a sad loss by the death of Captain A. E. Jones, its Grand Old Man. No other individual during the 100 years in which the Company has been